Multistakeholder Governance and Democracy

Multistakeholder governance is proposed as the way forward in global governance. For some leaders in civil society and government who are frustrated with the lack of power of the UN system and multilateralism it is seen as an attractive alternative; others, particularly in the corporate world, see multistakeholder governance as offering a more direct hand and potentially a legitimate role in national and global governance.

This book examines how the development of multistakeholderism poses a challenge to multilateralism and democracy. Using a theoretical, historical perspective it describes how the debate on global governance evolved and what working principles of multilateralism are under threat. From a sociological perspective, the book identifies the organizational beliefs of multistakeholder groups and the likely change in the roles that leaders in government, civil society, and the private sector will face as they evolve into potential global governors. From a practical perspective, the book addresses the governance issues which organizations and individuals should assess before deciding to participate in or support a particular multistakeholder group.

Given the current emphasis on the participation of multiple actors in the Sustainable Development Goals, this book will have wide appeal across policy-making and professional sectors involved in negotiations and governance at all levels. It will also be essential reading for students studying applied governance.

Harris Gleckman is Senior Fellow of the Center on Governance and Sustainability, University of Massachusetts Boston, and Director of Benchmark Environmental Consulting, USA. Dr Gleckman has also been a participant for over twenty years in international economic and environmental negotiations and a consultant to intergovernmental organizations, transnational corporations, and civil society organizations. He is the former Chief of the New York office of UNCTAD, Project Planning Officer for the first UN Financing for Development Conference, and Chief of the Environmental Unit of the UN Centre on Transnational Corporations.

"The understanding of how the management of global and regional transborder issues and problems are addressed has evolved considerably over the past decade. No longer an exclusive preserve of diplomats and international lawyers focussing on formal institutional arrangements and legal instruments the scope has widened to encompass a rapidly growing set of issue areas and multitude of new actors from civil society and the corporate world. Harris Gleckman's book is a significant contribution in mapping the evolution from hierarchical legal exegesis and intergovernmental power play towards more supple horizontal relations between a diverse and expanding set of stakeholders. The author does this with the rare combination of the clarity of the sharp analyst and the insights of a seasoned participant in these processes. His book is essential reading for anyone involved in the changing patterns of global governance." – *Peter Hansen, former Executive Director of the Commission on Global Governance and Under-Secretary-General for Humanitarian Affairs*

"Dr. Gleckman has written the definitive critique of the current 'non-system' of international global governance, and of the emergent multistakeholder groups seeking to fill the gaps in the former. Gleckman then ventures beyond analysis to propose criteria essential for any just, inclusive, accountable and effective institutions that would address global crises. This volume is addressed to all intelligent and ethical people concerned about global problems and committed to the quality of their resolution." – *Jo Marie Griesgraber, Executive Director, New Rules for Global Finance, USA*

"An invaluable and comprehensive analysis of contemporary challenges to multilateralism as the organizing principle for global governance. With piercing precision Gleckman identifies gaps and limitations in governance and questions the illusion of democracy and participation. The book offers a welcome and thoughtful guide for improving decisionmaking and assuming responsibility in a context of distributed power." – *Maria Ivanova, Associate Professor of Global Governance, University of Massachusetts Boston, USA*

"*Multistakeholder Governance and Democracy* is a bracing journey through the rise and rise of multistakeholderism. Arguing from his unique inside experience that this new form of global governance has come not just to supplement, but to challenge, multilateralism, Harris Gleckman sounds the alarm on whether we need to radically respond to the proliferation of instruments that are neither founded on principles of inclusive democracy nor accountability. A powerful and gripping exploration of this significant yet little-known evolution in global power, which leaves readers with a powerful challenge: can we imagine a new or reform global governance system that addresses the inequities and power imbalances of globalization, while upholding principles of democracy, inclusion and accountability?" – *Amelia Evans, International Human Rights Lawyer and co-founder of The Institute for Multi-Stakeholder Initiative Integrity, USA*

"In this fascinating book, Harris Gleckman illuminates how multistakeholderism has rapidly become the go-to form of governance for global challenges, with corresponding implications on democracy, transparency, responsibility, and accountability. A must read for students and practitioners, and for citizens, whose rights and interests are increasingly subject to multistakeholder governance." – *Lisa Sachs, Director, Columbia Center on Sustainable Investment, Columbia Law School – The Earth Institute, Columbia University, USA*

Multistakeholder Governance and Democracy
A Global Challenge

Harris Gleckman

First published 2018
by Routledge
2 Park Square, Milton Park, Abingdon, Oxon OX14 4RN

and by Routledge
711 Third Avenue, New York, NY 10017

Routledge is an imprint of the Taylor & Francis Group, an informa business

© 2018 Harris Gleckman

The right of Harris Gleckman to be identified as author of this work has been asserted by him in accordance with sections 77 and 78 of the Copyright, Designs and Patents Act 1988.

All rights reserved. No part of this book may be reprinted or reproduced or utilized in any form or by any electronic, mechanical, or other means, now known or hereafter invented, including photocopying and recording, or in any information storage or retrieval system, without permission in writing from the publishers.

Trademark notice: Product or corporate names may be trademarks or registered trademarks, and are used only for identification and explanation without intent to infringe.

British Library Cataloguing-in-Publication Data
A catalogue record for this book is available from the British Library

Library of Congress Cataloging-in-Publication Data
Names: Gleckman, Harris, author.
Title: Multistakeholder governance and democracy : a global challenge / Harris Gleckman.
Description: New York, NY : Routledge, 2018. | Includes bibliographical references and index.
Identifiers: LCCN 2018022988| ISBN 9781138502109 (hardback) | ISBN 9781138502130 (pbk.) | ISBN 9781315144740 (ebook)
Subjects: LCSH: Intergovernmental cooperation. | Government policy.
Classification: LCC JZ1318 .G552 2018 | DDC 320.6–dc23
LC record available at https://lccn.loc.gov/2018022988

ISBN: 978-1-138-50210-9 (hbk)
ISBN: 978-1-138-50213-0 (pbk)
ISBN: 978-1-315-14474-0 (ebk)

Typeset in Sabon
by Wearset Ltd, Boldon, Tyne and Wear

Printed and bound in Great Britain by
TJ International Ltd, Padstow, Cornwall

Contents

List of tables	x
Preface	xi
Acknowledgments	xviii
List of abbreviations	xix

1 Multilateralism and multistakeholderism: global governance gaps   1

Introduction 1
Structural limitations of contemporary multilateralism 2
   On global ecology 3
   On global finance 4
   On global inequities 4
Global governance and the next generation of democratic standards 5
Democracy and global governance gaps 6
Multistakeholderism and representative democracy 7
Multistakeholderism and the rule of law 10
Multilateralism and multi-constituency consultations 12
From multi-constituency consultations to multistakeholder governance 14
Diversity of internal structures of multistakeholder governance groups 16
Types of multistakeholder governance groups 16
   Policy-oriented multistakeholder governance groups 16
   Product and process-oriented (standard-setting) multistakeholder groups 17
   Project-oriented multistakeholder groups 23

vi *Contents*

2 **How did we get here? A convergence of multiple trends**   28

   Macro political-economic factors 29
      Proliferation of major unresolved international crises 29
      Perception of multilateralism as a dysfunctional system 30
      Weakening of the nation-states' ability to manage globalization and to protect the global ecosystem 32
      The rise of authoritarianism invites an appeal to a socially-wider decision-making system 33
   Structural transformations 34
      Transformation of the relationship between TNCs and the UN system 34
      Transformation of the relationship between NGOs/CSOs and the UN system 37
      Transformation of the relationship between CSOs and TNCs 38
      Transformation of the corporate belief that the management of globalization may need a global quasi-state function 40
   Recognition of multistakeholderism as a governance form 42
      The evolution of "stakeholder" as a concept of governance 42
      The birth of elite corporate bodies with a multistakeholder perspective 45
      First movers deemed successful 46
      Welcoming by the intergovernmental system of multi-constituency consultations and non-state global leadership 47
   Macro-forces creating a new political platform for global governance 48

3 **Global actors from multilateralism to multistakeholderism**   52

   Governance actors from yesterday to tomorrow 52
   The institutional foundation for global governance 53
      Intergovernmental structures 55
      Special governance arrangements under multilateralism 57
      Intergovernmental bodies and their secretariats 58
      Multilateralism and non-state actors 59
      Non-governmental organizations/civil society organizations 59

The private sector and multilateralism 61
New actors in multistakeholder governance 63
   Transition process from multilateralism to multistakeholderism 63
   A new governance role: the convener 65
   Changed role for state actors in the new global governance system 71
   Changed role of the UN system secretariats as independent actors in global governance 73
   Changed role for civil society organizations in global governance 74
   Changed role of private sector actors in global governance 76
   Donors adapt to multistakeholderism 78
   Other non-state actors become participants in governance under multistakeholderism 78

4 Structural and institutional characteristics of multistakeholderism   **83**

Nine beliefs and their governance consequences 84
   Unsolved global problems 84
   "Stakeholders" as a meaningful governance category 86
   The ability to identify all relevant stakeholders 87
   A participant brings the support of their organization or sector 89
   Volunteerism as a necessary condition 90
   Equitable decision-making 92
   Managing conflicts of interest 93
   Enhanced efficiency and effectiveness 95
   On transparency 97
Structural and institutional characteristics of multistakeholder governance 99
   The one-big-table model 99
   A decision-making body explicitly weighted by stakeholder categories 100
   A governing council elected from stakeholder chambers 102
   A governing council advised by stakeholder chambers 103
   International secretariat-led multistakeholder groups 104

Multistakeholder bodies parallel to intergovernmental
bodies 106
Replacement government in failed states 107
Chapter summary 108

5   A detailed guide to decision-making about a
    multistakeholder group   111

*Four questions on the composition of a multistakeholder
group* 113
#1 Are all the appropriate categories of participants
reflected in the multistakeholder group? 113
#2 What internationally recognized criteria should be used
to select a legitimate organization to represent a
stakeholder category or to select an individual
representative within these organizations? 114
#3 How should an organization be designated for each
stakeholder category and how should individuals be
selected to represent each participating
organization? 116
#4 What should be the overall diversity balance for a
multistakeholder group? 117
Four questions on internal governance 119
#1 Are the terms of reference for the group clear and
acceptable? 119
#2 How will decision-making operate within the
multistakeholder group? 121
#3 What should be the dispute resolution system for a
multistakeholder group? 123
#4 What procedures should be followed to decide to close a
multistakeholder group? 124
Three questions on external responsibilities 125
#1 How should an organization in a multistakeholder
group engage with others in its designated stakeholder
group and how should an individual participant engage
with her/his organization? 125
#2 What should be the reporting and disclosure
standards to the general public and the multilateral
system? 126
#3 How should the multistakeholder group engage with
the wider community on closure or a potential
closure? 128

Two questions on financial responsibility 129
   #1 Where are the resources coming from to pay for the operating expenses of the multistakeholder group, and, separately, where are the resources coming from to finance the programs and/or the recommendations of the multistakeholder group? 129
   #2 How are decisions made on where resources will go to underwrite the program as well as to satisfy organizational needs? 130
Chapter summary 131

6 **Where can we go from here?**   134

The current state of play 134
Multistakeholderism: additional structural limitations 136
Next steps on the governance of multistakeholderism 137
Next steps on global democratic governance 138
   Re-constituting multilateralism 138
   Directly governing diverse power sources 140
   A new organizing unit for global governance 140
Concluding observations 141

Index   143

Tables

1.1	Examples of mis-labelling traditional multi-constituency consultations as multistakeholder meetings	13
1.2	Examples of global policy-oriented multistakeholder groups	18
1.3	Examples of environmental and social standard-setting multistakeholder groups	20
1.4	Examples of high-impact technology standard-setting multistakeholder groups	22
1.5	Examples of global project-oriented multistakeholder groups	24
3.1	Examples related to the diversity of categories of stakeholders	67
3.2	Potential stakeholder categories for a multistakeholder-based governance system	68
3.3	Diversity of the number of categories of stakeholders in a multistakeholder governance group	70
4.1	Examples of assertions that all relevant stakeholders participate in a multistakeholder group	88
4.2	Examples of calls for volunteer participation by multistakeholder groups	91

Preface

I was a UN staff member from the late 1970s to mid-2000s and participated in a range of global economic and environmental governance issues while working in the former UN Centre on Transnational Corporations, the Secretary-General's Office at UNCTAD, the Office for Financing for Development in the UN Department of Economic Affairs, and in UNCTAD's New York office. Over this time period I watched as certain governments pushed the multilateral system to take positive steps to address climate change, to introduce the role of transnational corporations into global debate, to link environment and economics more closely together, to disclose a list of products that were banned or severely restricted in one country but then sold in other countries, and many other ground-breaking initiatives.

Unfortunately, I also watched over this period as governments at the UN backed away from trying to manage globalization. Further, following the initial effort to grapple with scientific assessments of the causes of climate change, I watched governments reverse course and fail to prevent massive anthropogenic impacts on the planet's ecosystem. I also watched as global poverty worsened, wars continued, and new ones were waged while the multilateral system's best contributions was all too often well-worded declarations.

In retrospect, one of the early transformations toward a multistakeholder world occurred in 2002 when I participated in planning two intergovernmental processes – the Financing for Development Conference in Monterrey, Mexico, and the 10th anniversary conference of the Rio Earth Summit in Johannesburg, South Africa. At these meetings "stakeholders" were given a special category in global governance.

In 2007, after retiring from the United Nations, the Institute for Environmental Security at The Hague asked me to head a project looking at how the major national and international economic institutions were constraining other parts of governments which were trying to conclude an effective climate agreement. The senior advisors to this study all raised the need to look at a new form of global governance as one part of organizing the world to tackle climate change.

xii *Preface*

At the end of 2009, I served in the office of the Executive Director of the 2009 Copenhagen Conference of the Parties to the UNFCCC climate convention. In the months beforehand, governments and the UN saw the real possibility of a binding climate agreement. The possibility disappeared as volunteerism, a key feature of multistakeholderism, took center stage with the leading governments endorsing the voluntary Copenhagen Accord.

In reaction to the start of the 2008/2009 Global Recession, the World Economic Forum (WEF) from a quite different perspective saw the need for a major re-examination of global governance. The WEF project, called the Global Redesign Initiative (GRI), was under the direct leadership of its three top officials. The GRI project involved 700 participants over a one-and-half year period and concluded with recommendations on what they believed should be the next form of global governance (WEF 2010). The GRI report was clearly a ground-breaking report with a strong theoretical argument for multistakeholderism. The beneficial claim of multistakeholderism was supported by sixty sector-specific policy recommendations.

Thanks to a chance remark from a former UN colleague, I started to read the WEF report. In multilateral circles, in international social movements, and in multistakeholder groups striving to introduce ethical, social, and environmental guidelines into global markets, no one seemed to have noticed this strategic governance proposal. Working with the Center of Governance and Sustainability at UMass-Boston, I drafted a long interactive website that served as a Readers' Guide and a critique of the GRI (Gleckman 2012). I shared with WEF that a new form of global governance was necessary; what I didn't share with them was that multistakeholderism should be the basis for the next form of global governance.

Looking around the international landscape, it was clear that the early steps toward a new global governance system based on multistakeholderism were finding institutional support. Today, when a new challenge appears on the global agenda, governments and other international actors are very likely to call for a multistakeholder group (MSG) to address the challenge rather than establish a multilateral body to address the crisis. If a community sees a need for a global standard to evaluate products produced in a gender-sensitive manner, they are more likely to propose a multistakeholder standard-setting body than turn to UN Women or UNCTAD. If another community or a transnational corporation (TNC) aspires to clean up a river basin, they are more likely to locate other local "stakeholders" and create a "public-private partnership" to repair the riparian district, rather than lobby a legislature to protect the river. When the General Assembly in 2015 adopted the Sustainable Development Goals, governments formally committed themselves to "enhance the global partnership for sustainable development, complemented by multistakeholder partnerships that mobilize and share knowledge, expertise, technology and financial resources, to support the achievement of the sustainable development goals in all countries, in particular developing countries" (UN 2015).

Multistakeholderism is a different organizational and institutional arrangement than the international governance system established at the end of World War I or World War II. Multistakeholder global governance is based on a different allocation of power and a different conception of democracy. In multilateralism, governments, as representative of their citizens, take the final decisions on global issues and direct international organizations to implement these decisions. In multistakeholderism, "stakeholders" become the central actors. Decision-making and the implementation of these global decisions are often disconnected from the intergovernmental sphere. While the MSG may cite a multilateral goal that it asserts it is implementing on behalf of governments, an MSG has no obligation to report its activities to – or to take instructions from – the intergovernmental community. Consequently, concepts such as "representative," "rule of law," "election of delegates," and "state sovereignty" no longer follow the same principles as in the multilateral system.

In effect, the multistakeholder approach argues that the correct way forward is to bring together all the global actors that have a potential "stake" in an issue and ask them to collaboratively sort out a solution. The presumption is that this configuration of actors with their combined capacities will best be able to figure out how to act. In this scenario, the participation of nation-states in a given MSG is problematic. Some nation-states, but not all of them, are invited to join the multistakeholder process, if in the mind of the group's convener and other founders the nation-state in question has a "stake" in the issue.

What is overlooked in the pragmatism surrounding the governance viability of multistakeholderism is the governance of the approach itself, and specifically the governance rules that bring together organizations, governments, and individuals which are said to have a "stake" in an issue. This book treats multistakeholderism as one potential candidate to be the next foundation of global governance. It does this by explaining both the decision-making process and power characteristics within multistakeholder governance arrangements and the external power relationships of these multistakeholder arrangements. It also examines elementary issues of responsibility, obligation, liability, accountability, and transparency in global affairs.

Democratic governance principles and multistakeholderism

National democracies and intergovernmental multilateralism have developed a number of principles of governance and organizational structures to incorporate democratic principles. Even when these principles and organizational structures are distorted by power relationships, they provide a democracy-centered base from which one can appraise any future system of governance. There are clear contrasts at the international level between multilateralism and multistakeholderism and clear contrasts between national democratic principles and practices and those of multistakeholderism in domestic public-private partnerships. Multilateralism itself faces three fundamental challenges because of its foundation on the concept of nation-states. These contrasts and challenges are elaborated in Chapter 1.

In this book, the phrase "MSGs" or "multistakeholder projects" are used to identify individual multistakeholder undertakings, while "multistakeholderism" is used to reflect the theory of global governance exemplified by the use of multistakeholder projects or groups. These multistakeholder projects focus their attention on three different types of governance issues: some focus on developing policies, some on setting standards for international markets, and some on implementing time-limited projects. This three-part classification along with examples of each type of multistakeholder project completes the introduction to multistakeholder governance in Chapter 1.

The origins of multistakeholder governance proposals

Multistakeholderism did not appear overnight. Its evolution and development is the result of the convergence of twelve different phenomena over the past twenty-five years. These largely autonomous tracks have altered traditional political, economic, and ideological terrains and are quietly leading toward the institutional acceptability of multistakeholderism.

Some of the avenues to multistakeholder legitimation are, frankly, unexpected. For example, the US Department of Defense, which first created the internet and authorized domain names, and subsequently the US Department of Commerce were only willing to relinquish control to ICANN (the Internet Corporation for Assigned Names and Numbers), if there was a multistakeholder governance structure led by IT firms in place. The US Government's core concern regarding this requirement was that, if the US Government were to hand over the keys to governing the internet, it did not want any other government to be involved, even if an international organization already existed to coordinate multi-country communication systems. Another unexpected avenue toward multistakeholder governance was the world of gambling. A fuller discussion of the history of various forces that have brought multistakeholder governance into the international arena is provided in Chapter 2.

The evolution of new international actors

Over the past thirty years, government delegates have met at intergovernmental meetings with non-government representatives, who are convinced that they have every right to be included in negotiating processes. This includes the right to be heard by government representatives, not just as assertive lobbyists or technically competent experts, but as autonomous and independent political actors. In this light, representatives of women's organizations, advocates for cleaner seas, and spokespeople for better health care see themselves – and are seen by government representatives – not just as citizens of any given country. Rather, they are seen as legitimate and independent participants in the global governance community "representing" a part of the global ecosystem or a thematic community. Similarly, corporate executives advocating for free-market principles and business leaders seeking to convene a public-private solution to a problem see themselves – and are seen by government representatives – not just as commercial enterprises registered in one country but as a partners in public governance.

Rules over the past seventy-five years have been developed in the international arena to balance power relations between nation-states; now new rules are needed for multistakeholderism. Any new system of global governance that expects to be seen as legitimate will likely take many decades to devise basic rules which can reasonably balance inherent resource and power differences between the categories of actors in MSGs. Yes, making this happen is a challenging democratic exercise; however, at this stage in multistakeholder governance, it is not even on the agenda of most multistakeholder governance projects.

The advent of multistakeholderism means that the international community now has a proposal for an institutional structure that can complement or replace the centrality of the nation-state in global governance. Multistakeholderism is entering the global stage when nation-states face a challenging international issue or an issue where governments do not perceive they have the capacity to act or by inaction create a governance gap. Contemporary multistakeholderism however does not offer any clarity on how it will enhance global democracy. It also has not yet clarified how the current exclusive responsibilities and obligations of nation-states will shift when powerful non-state actors have a formal or semi-formal decision-making role in international relations.

Changes in the roles of global actors from multilateralism to multistakeholderism are explored further in Chapter 3.

Structural and institutional characteristics of multistakeholderism

The evolution of multistakeholder governance has occurred in parallel to the transformation of professional terminology in international affairs away from "international relations" toward "global governance." To be clear, multistakeholder global governance – even for its strongest advocates – is certainly not a world government in disguise. As multistakeholder governance is still in an experimental phase, current efforts made to articulate a formal definition may very well be getting ahead of the evolving reality.

At the moment, there are a series of commonly held beliefs by many participants and advocates of multistakeholder governance that underpin multistakeholderism and a series of different institutional arrangements used by MSGs. Some of these structural decision-making systems involve multiple chambers for different categories of stakeholders, while other institutional and structural systems involve creating a parallel governance system to UN system organizations (Gleckman 2013). These widely held beliefs and their complementary organizational arrangements are summarized in Chapter 4.

Assessment criteria about joining and/or approving a multistakeholder project

The issues facing decision-makers about multistakeholder governance are not simple, but rather are simultaneously highly technical and highly philosophical. After 400 years of nation-state governance and over seventy-five years of contemporary multilateralism, a good number of the assumptions about how global governance should work are no longer secure. The governance evolution toward multistakeholderism is occurring without any clarity about what its working democratic standards are or which global governance principles should guide decision-makers.

Chapter 5 attempts to distill the present knowledge about multistakeholderism and the governance choices that concerned leaders and scholars should reflect on when appraising when – or if – they will participate in or endorse a given MSG. It is also intended to contribute from a bottom-up perspective to the overall assessment of the democratic characteristics of multistakeholderism. The chapter is organized around thirteen thematic questions which were selected to aid in examining the governance process within a given MSG and democratic relations between the MSG and the wider world. This chapter, as the book itself, examines democracy and governance and, as such, does not address the comparative efficiency or effectiveness claims about multistakeholderism.

Breaking new ground

The foundation for the current multilateral structure was built over more than three years by government officials meeting in Washington, London, Dumbarton Oaks, Bretton Woods, and San Francisco. These discussions started in 1943 when it was not yet clear which forces were going to prevail in the battles of World War II (WWII).

Today a number of initiatives are underway to re-conceptualize global governance for the 21st century. These approaches are based on starkly different principles of and aspirations for global democracy. What is relevant, and this is elaborated on in Chapter 6, is that there are multiple options for the next phase of global governance.

The advent of multistakeholderism as a governance system is a challenge for the academy and for those working internationally to find the best way to solve a given international dilemma. From an academic standpoint, multistakeholderism with its assertion that multiple "stakeholders" are legitimate actors in governance sets it apart from prior international relations work. From a practitioner's perspective, understanding the democratic governance elements entailed by multistakeholderism is an essential component of an appraisal if their organization or agency is going to make a wise decision about whether to participate in or endorse a given multistakeholder project. And growing acceptance of multistakeholderism is a challenge for the wider global public who are seeking ways that they can influence international events that directly impact their daily lives.

I hope that this book can provide a framework for the assessment of global democracy and multistakeholderism for all these communities.

References

Gleckman, Harris. 2012. "Readers' Guide: Global Redesign Initiative." Boston: Center for Governance and Sustainability at the University of Massachusetts Boston. Available from www.umb.edu/gri.

Gleckman, Harris. 2013. "WEF Proposes a Public-Private United 'Nations.'" *Policy Innovations*. Accessed June 18, 2013. Available from www.carnegiecouncil.org/publications/archive/policy_innovations/commentary/000263.

UN. 2015. *Transforming our World: the 2030 Agenda for Sustainable Development*. GA Res 70/1, UN GA, 70th session, UN Doc A/RES/70/1 (October 21, 2015; adopted September 25, 2015).

WEF. 2010. "Global Redesign: Strengthening International Cooperation in a More Interdependent World." Geneva: World Economic Forum.

Acknowledgments

Over the past three years a number of people encouraged me to work on multistakeholder governance and the implications for global democracy. Without the support of Gonzalo Berrón, Brid Brennan, Pascale Burdon, Ben Collins, Jane Cottingham, Felix Dodds, Fiona Dove, Miriam Gleckman-Krut, Jo Marie Griesgraber, Peter Hansen, Maria Ivanova, Ron Kingham, Raphael Krut-Landau, Riva Krut, Craig Murphy, Andy Ross, Lisa Sachs, Flavio Valente, and Leslie Wade, this book would not have been written. It might not even have been attempted.

Friends and colleagues provided invaluable appraisals of draft chapters. I would like to sincerely thank Siobhan Airey, Brandon Brockmyer, Daniel Bornstein, Chantal Line Carpentier, Deval Desai, Amelia Evans, Rebecca DeWinter-Schmitt, Susan George, Khalil Hamdani, Nora McKeon, Heikki Patomaki, Rinalia Abdul Rahim, Ahmed Rhazaoui, and Sam Szoke-Burke for taking the time to comment on the drafts and letting me know when I was heading in the wrong direction.

I would like to extend thanks to MSI Integrity and Transnational Institute which invited me to share my developing ideas at their conferences in Amsterdam and San Francisco, and for their assistance in locating experts around the world who contributed to this endeavor.

I also want to thank two graduate researchers, Sarah Elizabeth Sharma and Mara Lipsou, who provided research assistance and support in finalizing the manuscript.

Even with all this advice and assistance, I take full responsibility for the arguments and evidence used in the book.

I have a special thanks to Tim Hardwick and Amy Louise Johnston at Routledge for agreeing to publish a book on multistakerholderism. Their understanding and cooperative spirit nurtured this author to finish this book.

Abbreviations

BRIC	an association of the governments of Brazil, Russia, India, and China
BWI	Bretton Woods Institutions
CEO	chief executive officer
COP	Conference of the Parties
CSD	Commission on Sustainable Development
CSO	civil society organization
CSR	corporate social responsibility
ECE	UN Economic Commission for Europe
ECOSOC	UN Economic and Social Council
EITI	Extractive Industries Transparency Initiative
FAO	Food and Agriculture Organization
FDI	foreign direct investment
FFD	Financing for Development
G20	Group of 20
G77	Group of 77 (developing countries)
GAVI	Global Vaccine Alliance
GRI	Global Redesign Initiative
ICANN	The Internet Corporation for Assigned Names and Numbers
ICC	International Chamber of Commerce
ICTI	International Council of Toy Industries
ILO	International Labour Organization
IMF	International Monetary Fund
ICoCA	International Code of Conduct for Private Security Providers' Association
IRENA	International Renewable Energy Agency
ISEAL	International Social and Environmental Accreditation and Labelling Alliance
ISO	International Organization for Standardization
ITU	International Telecommunication Union
IUCN	International Union for Conservation of Nature
MSG	multistakeholder group
NATO	North Atlantic Treaty Organization

NGO	non-governmental organization in consultative status with ECOSOC
NS&T	nanotechnology, science and technology
OECD	Organization for Economic Cooperation and Development
PPP	public-private partnership
SARS	severe acute respiratory syndrome
SDGs	Sustainable Development Goals
SE4ALL	Sustainable Energy for All
TNC	transnational corporation
UN	United Nations
UNCTAD	United Nations Conference on Trade and Development
UNCTC	United Nations Centre on Transnational Corporations
UNDP	United Nations Development Program
UNEP	United Nations Environment Programme
UNESCO	United Nations Educational Social and Cultural Organization
UNFCCC	United Nations Framework Convention on Climate Change
UNIDO	United Nations Development Organization
WCD	Commission on Dams
WEF	World Economic Forum
WHO	World Health Organization
WTO	World Trade Organization
WWF	World Wildlife Fund

1 Multilateralism and multistakeholderism

Global governance gaps

Introduction

A move to multistakeholderism would introduce a whole new set of governance actors and a new process for making global "laws and regulations." International multistakeholder bodies often have limited or adversarial connections to governments and intergovernmental bodies yet they function as if they are global governors (Avant et al. 2010). Multistakeholderism has also gained a degree of public acceptance as a new paradigm for global governance without the international community examining properly its legitimacy or effectiveness as an institution of governance. Some of these global governance arrangements initially started out closely associated with the UN system, such as the internet governance system, and have subsequently marginalized government involvement in their multistakeholder structure.

When Andy Potts writing in *The Economist* looked at 2016 internet governance proposals, he saw the beginnings of a replacement country:

> It will have a government (the organization's board), a constitution (its by-laws, which includes its mission and "core values"), a judiciary (an "independent review process," which leads to binding recommendations) and a citizenry of sorts (half-a-dozen "supporting organizations" and "advisory committees," which represent the different interest groups). These will have the right to kick out the board and block its budget.
>
> (Potts 2016)

In addition to political appeals for a multistakeholder governance system, there has been a proliferation of experiments in the practical realities of multistakeholder governance. The practices of these multistakeholder efforts, whether in setting voluntary standards for sustainable palm oil production or in devising programs to sustainably manage forests, are defining the characteristics of a potential new form of global governance.

All too often participants and proponents of multistakeholder governance opt to engage with these arrangements because they feel that governments and the UN system[1] are not efficient, effective, or expeditious in meeting their goals. This drive toward the pragmatic side of multistakeholderism, however, often leaves under-examined elements of the governance decision-making aspect of multistakeholderism. To put this evaluation in context, it is necessary also to recognize some the structural limitations of contemporary multilateralism.

Structural limitations of contemporary multilateralism

There is no shortage of global matters needing attention, some of which are a fundamental challenge to multilateralism as it operates today.

The existing backbone of international governance by the nation-state was born in the Westphalia peace conference of 1648. The conference began a process that established two crucial features of the nation-state in international relations. First, each nation state has sovereignty over its territory and domestic affairs to the exclusion of all external powers. The boundaries of one country indicated that its rulers, then appropriately denominated by the regal term "sovereigns," had the recognized power to govern within their boundaries. Following this, sovereigns with militaries outside this national boundary agreed not to interfere with domestic matters, at least in principle. The second feature was democratic in nature: each state, no matter how large or how small, would be considered equal in international law.

In the context of Westphalia of 1648, contemporary multilateralism is a rather recent process. It had its birth only during WWII. Still, the world has changed significantly since then. Self-assertions of global leadership by various non-state actors; the expansion of the international market into a globalized economy; the abrupt change in the ratio of financial capital over productive capital in the global economy; the growth in power of transnational corporations (TNCs); military adventurism by major governments; and the intentional weakening and underfunding of the UN system – to mention some of the structural changes that have occurred through this period – have meant that institutions created at the end of WWII have been under tremendous strain. This strain is evident in multilateralism in a number of ways, including not even having the ability to manage even one of its founding functions: the maintenance of peace and security.

Following the lead of the Thatcher and Reagan administrations, a number of major governments domestically adopted a strong political commitment to market-based economics. Translated to the global level, this ideology resulted in government delegates at UN system bodies increasingly stepping back from even attempting to govern the negative effects of globalization. Into this abandoned political space, TNCs have successfully expanded their political and economic reach. TNCs and corporate executives see the nation-state as a minor actor in the governance of globalization and therefore similarly see the multilateral system as a junior player in global governance.[2] At the same time TNCs consider themselves and the free market to be legitimate actors in setting global agendas and in creating solutions for global problems, even ones that they may have a hand in causing. The net result is that a good number of global economic and social issues lack an institutional home in the multilateral system.

On global ecology

On the global ecological side, multilateralism has a political-geographic structural challenge. Countries are defined fundamentally by land boundaries;[3] however, many global ecological matters are situated beyond the borders that define the scope of authority of governments. For example, the regulation of plastic products used around the world that collect in massive ocean piles are simply outside the policy and legal jurisdictions of land-based countries. There are a large number of similar global and regional crises that are hard to govern as two-thirds of the planet consists of international waters and a dynamic atmosphere exists far above national overflight boundaries. Further, many anthropogenic effects on the atmosphere are felt beyond state land boundaries where emissions are produced and a significant share of the ecological threats to biodiversity come from outside a nation's territorial boundaries.

Multilateral governance systems surrounding the environment have been stymied when a number of governments agree that an issue is a matter of collective importance, but the relevant pollution-producing government does not share the same view. For example, while the international community looks at the Amazon as the "lungs of the world," Brazil often sees this as sovereign territory to be developed as Brazilians alone see fit. Similarly, the US and other developed countries consider that their rate of release of greenhouse gas is fundamentally a national matter, not one where the international community should have decision-making capacity.

In some cases, governments find creative solutions around this limitation. National governments have negotiated, for example, an agreement on "straddling and migratory fish" to reflect that some species breed in one country's waters while they are caught in another. They have agreed that far-offshore oil rigs are governed by the country where they are registered even if it is hundreds of miles away. However, broader agreements, such as the Convention on the Law of the Sea, have been not effective in overcoming this land-based governance limitation, given that it is primarily concerned with mining rights and the movement of naval and commercial shipping rather than managing the global ocean commons.

4 *Multilateralism and multistakeholderism*

On global finance

The 2008/2009 financial crisis highlighted to billions of individuals around the world as well as to multinational banks, national monetary authorities, and business-oriented associations that contemporary multilateralism, governments and influential business authorities did not have the capacity to adequately govern the current global financial system. The trigger for this crisis – a housing finance crisis and a brokerage house collapse in one country – spread around the world in a matter of days, and no authority was able to adequately slow its transmission. In most previous financial crises, concerns focused on the ability for liberalized capital to abruptly move in and out of a country. After 2008, however, this concern was seen as secondary to a wider recognition that the entire international financial system may be unstable and unmanageable even by the Group of Twenty (G20) financially significant governments. No one, except scholars and some officials from smaller developing countries, even considered that the multilateral system should have governance authority over such crises.[4]

Simultaneously, many TNCs and multinational banking entities have taken advantage of the jurisdictional boundaries of nation-states to engage in tax jurisdiction shopping, creating flags of convenience for corporate registrations and large-scale illicit offshore banking. The inability and unwillingness of nation-states to prevent other nation-states from conceding their sovereignty through such behaviors undermines the integrity of the financial system. Every effort is made by Organization for Economic Cooperation and Development (OECD) governments to open the door for the flexible movement of capital between nation-states. Unfortunately, these same governments have not made an equivalent effort to establish a reasonable global tax system, an equitable global currency system, or a transparent global business registration system. This contradiction between the rhetoric surrounding global financial governance and the realities of a globalized economy has resulted in a fragmented financial supervisory system based on the nation-state and unable to ensure global financial stability.

On global inequities

Sovereignty is the cornerstone of the Westphalian[5] global order. Individuals in the Westphalian world are involved in international affairs only because of their status as citizens of a particular nation-state. Yet people, with or without a sovereign's protection, can be negatively affected by global forces. The globalized economy has produced globalized inequalities, where people who are at the bottom or even in the middle income brackets in the globalized economy are excluded from meaningful participation in global governance, including on matters that they perceive affect them directly.

Macro-economic crises, global ecological crises, pandemic health crises, migration crises, and financial crises confront existing institutions of global governance with significant challenges. The structural split between the forms of contemporary global governance mirror the split between the globalized economy and the global inequalities in the world. If a global governance system does not grant a formal seat at the decision-making table to all, then there is no counter-balancing force to prevent the greater and faster growth of global economic and social inequalities.

Out of these perceptions and realities has grown the recognition in the international community and in communities around the world that some new, more effective and democratic global governance system is needed.

Global governance and the next generation of democratic standards

On the democratic side, the next system of global governance should improve upon the democratic practices built into multilateralism. A new system should embody not only long recognized democratic principles but also contemporary governance values and practices.

In 2014, the former President of Brazil, Fernando Henrique Cardoso, chaired a panel on non-state actors and the UN system. The panel report noted:

> Concerning democracy, a clear paradox is emerging: while the substance of politics is fast globalizing (in the areas of trade, economics, environment, pandemics, terrorism, etc.), the process of politics is not; its principal institutions (elections, political parties and parliaments) remain firmly rooted at the national or local level. The weak influence of traditional democracy in matters of global governance is one reason why citizens in much of the world are urging greater democratic accountability of international organizations.
>
> (Cardoso 2004: 8)

In multilateralism, there is now the general expectation that international secretariats, panels and research teams on any given issue should be gender-balanced. In multistakeholder practice, there may – or may not – be a discrete stakeholder representing women or LGBTQ communities. Even if there is a discrete gender-based stakeholder category or two, unless there are only one or two other categories in a particular MSG, the group as a whole cannot be gender-neutral. Rather, all stakeholder categories within an MSG would themselves need to be gender-balanced, which is currently not the case in any known MSG. A future democratic global governance system should thus be fashioned to resolve this form of gender governance inequality.

Intergovernmental groups and the UN system secretariat are as a matter of course expected to be geographically balanced. In MSGs, however, this is a non-essential feature. Some current MSGs have designated individuals from different geographic areas. Nevertheless, the definition of geographic regions varies from MSG to MSG. Particular regional groupings in an MSG, like North and South, are fundamentally unhelpful from a democratic perspective. There are far more people living in what is understood to be the "South" than in the "North," and this bi-regional categorization system omits all the countries that have been previously designated as in the "East European" region or were parts of the former USSR.

In a number of national democracies, election districts or outcomes should in one way or another be constructed to ensure that minority ethnic communities are not excluded from effective political participation. The stakeholder-based membership however makes it difficult to consider the ethnic identity or any similar identity categorization of the stakeholders in an MSG.

In traditional democratic theory, the core unit is the individual citizen, who can vote and provide their opinion on any given policy or action. A new global governance system needs to grapple with the lack of popular direct access to the global governance decision-making process. A stakeholder-based system is not structured to give appropriate centrality to individuals affected by its governance. Were this the case, then 80 percent of the composition of a legitimately constituted global policy MSG would consist of individuals from the "developing world" and most of them would be from India or China.

Strengthening democracy between peoples and nations may well be a necessary condition for the future stabilization of globalization. As such, this democratic goal should be a central element in the evaluation of multi-stakeholderism or any proposed new system of global governance.

Democracy and global governance gaps

The next generation of global governance will also need to take steps to solve a number of complex governance gaps. Multistakeholder proponents assert that multistakeholderism will in fact close a number of these significant governance gaps.

Some global governance gaps arise when governments avoid seeing or minimize seeing global risks, as when social inequality, societal violence and climate impacts drive populations to be involuntary migrants. In other cases, the risks are recognized but meaningful action is not taken, as when the multilateral system limits its response to a declaration or a non-binding resolution. The limited response is often made because there is a direct or indirect assertion by some major international actor that their institutions alone will take care of the problem and consequently the UN system should not take meaningful action. The G20 and the private sector, for example, make such assertions regarding managing the global finance system and regulating the international market.

The third form of global governance gaps is when one part of a government or one part of the UN system takes a minimal or no action response in order to avoid a direct fight with another part of that government (e.g., the trade department or central bank) or another part of the UN system. The organizational avoidance may be because the policy arm wants to avoid a battle with the financing arm of the government, or because organizational boundaries and tensions are seen as too contentious to be addressed. The fourth form of global governance gaps are those where there ought to be a specially focused organization to address a recognized global issue such as youth unemployment, addressable health care disparities or any of the three issues identified above, but the multilateral system has not established such an organization.

In spite of these governance gaps, current national democratic practice and democratic features of multilateralism are a useful baseline to assess how any new candidate for the next global governance system matches up. The choice of this baseline does not mean that multilateralism and national democratic practices represent some ideal form of democracy, but rather that they can act as a framework of reference against which to assess whether multistakeholderism or a particular MSG operates in a more or less democratic manner.

Multistakeholderism and representative democracy

In multistakeholderism, a small powerful sub-group of actors plus a "representative" set of state and non-state actors are invited to solve a pressing public issue and fix a governance gap. Each MSG needs at least one powerful non-state member, usually a TNC or two, to give the MSG the necessary appearance of clout to get off the ground and to replace the access to power represented by governments. On the other hand, an MSG does not routinely include leaders from impoverished communities, national trade unionists, leaders of indigenous nations, international groups of involuntary migrants, or spokespersons from Southern social movements.

In practice, an MSG is generally started by a convener who reaches out to others to become members of the group. In multistakeholder language, these potential members are called "representatives" of particular social communities or social-ecological concerns. As the convener has a major role in selecting the individual members of a group, in democratic terms it would be more accurate to call the individuals brought together as "designee spokespersons," rather than "representatives." And, as their designee status is internal to any given MSG, these organizations and individuals have no clear obligation to consult with others who share their specified concern or community. Proponents of multistakeholderism also assert that, "everyone with a stake is involved" or "all relevant stakeholders" are engaged with a given MSG. These assertions are often advanced as supplemental evidence that the multistakeholder process is an inclusive one. Yet given the way MSGs are established, it is probably more accurate to describe an MSG as an exclusive body, not as an inclusive one.

Some advocates of multistakeholder governance assert that "participatory governance" is clearly better than any form of state-centered or intergovernmental governance, as there are more and different types of actors in the room. These additional stakeholders, they assert, "represent" better social or ecological concerns (e.g., biodiversity, marine mammals, ageism, or anti-racism) or more effectively bring conceptual communities to the table (e.g., women's groups, people down river from a project, indigenous communities).[6] Yet there is no clear way to assign a representative category to a specific non-human constituency or to a conceptually defined social community. For instance, in the field of rights-based constituencies, there are a wide range of views regarding what "human rights" entail. In addition, there is an equally legitimate argument that each separate "human right" should have a distinct stakeholder category. In the case of designating a person from a given social community, there is, for example, no international women's body that could elect its individual representatives to participate in an MSG and little agreement about whether the views of elderly women, women workers, women in rural China or LGBTQ women could be conveyed by a single women's representative.

Global social, economic, gender, or environmental concepts and the realities they are associated with are simply not unambiguous in character; they are each complex in their own right and in their interactions with each other. In national democracies, a great deal of attention is given to drawing carefully – for good or not so good – reasons the boundaries of election districts. In multistakeholder governance arrangements there is no unambiguous way to create meaningful bounds around a large number of potential stakeholder categories and their sub-categorizations. In spite of these difficulties – or maybe because of them – some proponents of representing these categories largely dismiss these concerns and assert that, if they didn't take on the representation of human rights or other categories, no one else would.

In effect, the convener-based appointment process is one of the new features of multistakeholder governance and one that inherently limits the democratic character of an MSG. The use of "representative-" based vocabulary as well as claims to involve "all relevant stakeholders" seeks to imbue multistakeholderism with a democratic character in order to give the process, as this book argues later, an illusion of democracy.

The option for resolving certain gaps in global governance and certain global problems are effectively limited using a multistakeholder form of governance. Those global matters which are structural to world capitalism, such as racism or global income inequities, are not likely to be amenable to solutions within a multistakeholder governance system. Similarly, some other global solutions which involve non-market-based mechanisms are effectively excluded as potential solutions, as most MSGs include a dominant TNC member.

Even with these two significant exemptions, there remain a good number of global governance matters that currently need global attention and are currently proposed for multistakeholder governance. For example, at the moment there are at least forty-six international standard-setting MSGs addressing the moral vacuum in product markets. In 2017, the World Economic Forum (WEF) identified thirty-five globally important policy issues that they assigned to one of their multistakeholder Global Future Councils (WEF 2017).

The advent of multistakeholderism on the international stage has followed on the US Supreme Court's decision to grant personhood to corporations. Corporate personhood grants to legally licensed firms some elements of a citizen's right to participate in governance. The acceptance of multistakeholder governance moves beyond corporate personhood and in effect endorses the concept of stakeholder personhood. In multistakeholderism, corporations and other stakeholders are asserting that they have a legitimate right to participate in global governance. In doing so, they are creating a new status for a wide range of institutions and organizations, which assert that they are authorized to make public policy decisions as if they were persons, citizens or governments.

The core standard for a representative national democracy is captured in the phrase "one person one vote." At the intergovernmental level the analogous statement is "one country one vote." While there are clearly exceptions, the governance arrangement at the General Assembly of the UN and the governing bodies of its specialized agencies and programs is based on this one-country-one-vote principle. No equivalent statement exists in the multistakeholder world. The WEF's Global Redesign Initiative (GRI) asserts in its first of five steps to a multistakeholder world that volunteerism and multistakeholder decision-making should take priority over the classical nation-state authority. The GRI authors proffer that this new approach should:

> ... redefine the international system as constituting a wider, multifaceted system of global cooperation in which intergovernmental legal frameworks and institutions are embedded as a core, but not the sole and sometimes not the most crucial, component.
>
> (WEF 2010: 7)

Multistakeholderism in another fashion is un-moored from key institutions inside governments. No longer is a department of state, a foreign office, or an economic ministry the lead force coordinating government participation in global governance. Under the leadership of a multistakeholder convener, the convener and leading members of an MSG have a disproportionate ability to designate which office from a national government is going to be involved, which official from a state or province is upgraded to having a government seat at a global conference, and which municipal officer is seated next to a national government official in an international meeting. For national government officials accustomed to asserting that they alone have the authority to represent a country's citizens, multistakeholderism can feel at times a little unsettling. If a national government is not seen as representing a country's citizens, what is the reason they are participating in finding solutions to global problems though a multistakeholder process?

Multistakeholderism raises a number of other challenging political questions. How does one intervene if the MSG with a credible constellation of actors and a good public disclosure policy sets out in the wrong direction? What are the platforms for contesting or reversing the direction? What if the actions of a multistakeholder governance group might harm a constituency that was not in the room? How does that constituency get itself invited to participate in future multistakeholder meetings or appeal the multistakeholder decisions? In democratic countries, there is the possibility of new elections, a recall petition, court cases, or parliamentary hearings to call on the state to justify its actions and to shift direction. For an international multistakeholder governance group, no recognized platform exists to challenge the composition of an MSG or to query the impact of their programs or actions. The lack of a dispute resolution mechanism or a quasi-judicial system sets multistakeholderism apart from government practices in democratic countries and from multilateralism.

Multistakeholderism and the rule of law

The 400-year evolution of international public law is being upended by multistakeholderism. Multistakeholder-based governance represents a decisive change in the ground rules for legitimate global decision-making and international action. Over the past centuries, the international community has developed a complex web of legal standards for judging state behavior. Customary international public law and practices, declarations and resolutions of intergovernmental bodies, and standards established through the adoption of treaties and conventions determine what are state obligations, responsibilities and liabilities. This web of the "rule of law" in international affairs is complemented by a range of related legal principles. With the advent of multistakeholderism, these state-based definitions of obligation, responsibility, liability, and other legal governance terms may well need to be reformulated to capture the new roles of global governors.

As an example of the changes in major governance definitions that may be needed, one may consider the scope of the concept of "conflict of interest." In national and multilateral circles a conflict of interest is said to occur when one party with a potential personal or financial benefit in the outcome of a public authority's decision participates in making that decision. In some situations, a conflict of interest is said to exist when the individual has a close family member that might benefit from the decision or when the public official has received an undisclosed payment from a potentially affected party. The object of these national practices is to prevent self-dealing or the perception of self-dealing by a public official, which would weaken democratic institutions and the public acceptance of fairness.

Transferring the idea of conflict of interest to the multistakeholder world, one could argue that a TNC executive should not be allowed to participate in an MSG if the decision or actions by that MSG could be financially beneficial to the executive's firm. Were this simple variant of a national definition used, it would exclude from an MSG all corporate executives whose income from the related business activity could impact their compensation. It may or may not permit executives from other parts of that TNC from participating, providing there is an effective "Chinese wall" between business units. In the case of public-private partnerships, business firms seem to be co-opting the very concept of conflict of interest. The firms involved in public-private partnerships assert in effect that conflict of interest standards should not apply to them, as they seek to resolve a local or global governance gap, even if their participation is conditioned on an outcome that is highly profitable to them.

From a different perspective, as MSGs function in the governance domain, there may be a need for a supplemental definition of "conflict of interest." For instance, if the potential solution to a governance gap an MSG proposes entails a choice between a market-based solution and a non-market-based solution, then one might need to reflect whether this political choice introduces a different form of conflict of interest for a corporate executive.

The complexity in the definition and scope of conflict of interest rules regarding operations in the multistakeholder context may in fact be easier to resolve than the changes needed in the understanding of international "obligations," "responsibilities," and "liabilities" as they relate to an MSG itself or to the individual participants in an MSG. If multistakeholderism is going to lead in "solving" global problems, are all the participants – or some of the participants – in a multistakeholder governance arrangement required to take on the obligations, responsibilities and liabilities previously recognized as expected of a nation-state? Does the nation-state lose some degree of responsibility and liability regarding the governance of an issue area, if they are no longer the sole recognized decision-makers in that area?

In some ways, proponents of the democratic legitimacy of multistakeholderism have attempted to preempt this reconsideration. Rather than focusing on a stakeholder's potential responsibilities, obligations and liabilities, they have declared that volunteerism is an intrinsic feature of multistakeholderism. This volunteerism includes the ability to join and the ability to withdraw whenever an individual stakeholder wishes. Besides other potential consequences of an international governance system built on such a transitory structure, volunteerism seeks to undercut any formal obligations or liabilities that might ensue from an action or omission by an MSG.

In contemporary international law, the traditional agent bound by hard and soft law is the nation-state. The nation-state can and cannot act in certain ways in relation to foreign nation-states and the citizens and enterprises of these states. As TNCs are now key actors in global governance, in due time international hard and soft law covering direct obligations, responsibilities, and liabilities may very well similarly extend to the TNCs participating in an MSG. More broadly, all stakeholders may become subject to direct obligations, responsibilities, and liabilities. Unless direct obligations are appropriately redesigned to include the stakeholders in multistakeholderism, the legal authority of nation-state obligations, responsibilities, and liabilities could diminish, introducing a new level of vagueness into public accountability.

Multilateralism and multi-constituency consultations

Multistakeholder governance is not the same as *multi-constituency consultations* hosted by government or the UN system. The practice of *multi-constituency consultations* is a long-standing tradition in domestic democratic governance systems. Examples of these processes include public hearings, public comment periods, town meetings, expert roundtable discussions, and constituent question and answer sessions. Soliciting the views of non-state actors from a very wide diversity of constituencies is well within traditional democratic practice, as the exchange explicitly or implicitly recognizes the primacy of the nation-state. At the international level *multi-constituency consultations* undoubtedly help intergovernmental bodies make better informed decisions. For example, the *multi-constituency consultative* processes at the High-Level Political Forum on Sustainable Development or the World Health Assembly have demonstrated that governments working multilaterally can make better informed decisions after hearing directly from key international constituencies.

It is a fortunate and long overdue development in the global arena that *multi-constituency consultative* arrangements are now welcomed as a routine part of normal intergovernmental deliberations. Only twenty-five years ago, this was not a common practice.

It is unfortunate however from an analytic and political perspective that these intergovernmentally convened *multi-constituency consultations* are called *multistakeholder arrangements*. The basis for this terminological confusion is that the UN system's use of multistakeholder language was borrowed incorrectly from the corporate management and government administrative management worlds (see Chapter 2 for a history of the term "stakeholder"). However, international intergovernmental bodies are analogous to national parliaments and congresses, not to business or government administrative offices. And congresses and parliaments tend to use public hearings, constituent question and answer sessions, or town meetings to describe engagements with their constituents, which does not reflect stakeholder-based terminology.

This book differentiates between *multi-constituency consultations* that bring together actors to work under a governmental or an intergovernmental authority and *multistakeholder governance* arrangements that strike out on their own to address a global or regional problem with relative or absolute autonomy from an intergovernmental body or a government. The distinction is quite important from a theoretical perspective as well as a practical one. A *multi-constituency consultative* arrangement works under the authority of nation-states and takes its frame of reference from a governmental or UN system body. On the other hand, a *multistakeholder governance* arrangement acts in a manner that is largely independent of a public governance system.

In the international community, the mis-labelling of these traditional *multi-constituency* engagement processes as *multistakeholder* consultations creates an intellectual and political history for governance by multistakeholder bodies. Table 1.1 has examples of this mis-labelling.

Table 1.1 Examples of mis-labelling traditional multi-constituency consultations as multistakeholder meetings

Organization	Scope of act	Description of structure
United Nations Forum on Forests	Promotes sustainable management and development of forests	A MultiStakeholder Dialogue (MSD) provides an opportunity for dialogue between Member States of the UNFF and representatives of Major Groups on issues relevant to UNFF sessions.
UN – High Level Political Forum	Follow up and review mechanism of the 2030 Sustainable Development Agenda	Major stakeholder groups representing NGOs, non-profit organizations, business and industry are assigned a consultative role and are invited to participate, submit documents, make recommendations, organize events and round tables.
FAO Committee on Food Security (CFS)	Issues of food security and nutrition	[CFS] is the foremost inclusive international and intergovernmental platform for all stakeholders to work together to ensure food security and nutrition for all.

Sources in order cited: United Nations Forum on Forests n.d.; UN n.d.; FAO Committee on World Food Security n.d.

14 *Multilateralism and multistakeholderism*

From multi-constituency consultations to multistakeholder governance

A group of civil society organizations (CSOs) teaming up together to address a global issue is an alliance of CSOs. A collection of TNCs working together is a trade association. A collection of governments working together is a regional or global multilateral effort. A meeting of foundation executives to address a growing global problem can be considered a collaboration of foundations. There are many other forms of *multi-constituency* engagement. When a CSO is contracted by an OECD government to advise on a development project, the resulting partnership is a normal government-civil society cooperative arrangement. When a scholar, a corporate executive, a government official, and a leader of a local CSO have a facilitated discussion, it can best be described as a seminar or a brainstorming session.

If a problem area can be solved by governments with their own resources, power, and with the willingness of other governments to work collaboratively, there is no need for an MSG. Similarly, when a TNC perceives that a problem needs addressing and it has adequate resources, power, and other TNCs willing to work jointly to tackle the issue, it is far more likely to engage with its peers in a trade association, rather than opt to create an MSG. Finally, international civil society organizations can join together in a global alliance of non-state, non-commercial organizations to define a global policy agenda and to influence the directions of other key actors without the alliance becoming a multistakeholder governance group.

Two key factors seem to mark the transition from a *multi-constituency consultation* group to a *multistakeholder governance* group. In an MSG, there is a shared recognition of relative power differences between the various participants. Power comes in many forms, including financial power, legitimacy power, human capital power, armed power, and moral power. All categories of actors and all types of governance powers participating in a multistakeholder governance system are not created equal. The relative power of TNC executives, for instance, exceeds the power of national or international labor unions. The relative power of governments is far greater, both economically and militarily, than any combination of national or international citizen movements. The power of well-established international NGOs gives them more power than any individual national or local NGO. And the power of an individual academic in a multistakeholder body may rest on the strength of their arguments, while the power of a religious leader rests on the strength of their moral leadership and the institutional arrangements of their religious body. These imbalances in comparative power within an MSG are different in character from that which exists between large nation-states and small nation-states, as in an MSG the potential power of each separate stakeholder category as well as of individual institutional stakeholders are located along different axes.

These asymmetries of power create an enduring internal tension within any multistakeholder governance group.

A *multi-constituency group* becomes an MSG when multiple constituencies are willing to surrender a degree of their own unique power in order to gain the power and participation of other constituencies without a meaningful tie to a guiding multilateral process or government. This assembly is not composed of merely any constituencies, but includes those, who, in the eyes of the convener and the early participants of the groups, have a "stake" in the consequences of the unresolved global problem or a clear preference for a specific type of outcome of the effort. A coalition of organizations concerned about an issue becomes a multistakeholder governance group when that coalition includes sufficient variety of forms of power which have, again in the view of the sponsor and/or other participants, the requisite combinations of power and actors to influence the solution.

A second, and complementary, facet of power considers the recognition by one constituency that they have the institutional responsibility to act on a given topic, but they lack the capacity or the power to act alone. Even when the UN and its sister institutions take the lead in setting global social, economic, and ethical standards, they have a shared recognition that, currently, governments are not willing to commit the resources necessary to implement these aspirational policy standards. In this case, governments appeal to other constituencies as partners in delivery.

At the national level, government agencies join with TNCs, international CSOs, and other domestic actors in public-private partnerships when the government office believes it cannot manage or finance a given public necessity by itself. Governments' perceived responsibility to act – be it a legislative responsibility, a responsibility to avoid a liability, or a social responsibility to do good – and the self-declared incapacity to deliver on that responsibility creates part of the political space for multistakeholderism. Governments with an obligation but without sufficient ability to act surrender a degree of power in order to gain what they perceive to be the capacities and powers of other constituencies.

In some of these situations, both governments and the UN system have recognized the global obligation to act but have stepped away from organizational leadership roles – or perhaps the multistakeholders have asserted such leadership – to the point where these bodies have morphed into decision-making actors that set aside original governmental or intergovernmental constituencies. In the area of corporate disclosure of environmental, social, and economic impacts, for example, the Global Reporting Initiative, which started with active support of the United Nations Environment Programme (UNEP), now has a relatively marginal committee to hear the views of governments.

MSGs created by senior officials of the UN system have a complicated character. They are inside and outside a UN organization. They are inside in the sense that they are under the personal responsibility of a senior UN Secretariat official. And they are outside in the sense they are not authorized or supervised by an intergovernmental body. The Global Compact, for example, is located in the Office of the Secretary-General but it only provides ex post reports to the General Assembly.

Diversity of internal structures of multistakeholder governance groups

Organizations participating in multistakeholder governance arrangements vary widely in their internal structures and the terminology they use to describe their structures. In this book, the terms "organization" and "institution" should be taken as shorthand for the variety of institutional arrangements that function in governments, the business community, civil society, religious bodies, social movements, academic departments, and other communities. For instance, an institution in the religious world may be an international federation of national churches or an inter-faith council in a given region; and an organization in the academic world may be a recognized university, an international scientific body, or an international professional association. Similarly, the word "agency" in this book should be taken as shorthand for an office associated with an organization or institution.

Also in this book, the terms "leaders" and "heads of organizations" should be taken to mean the relevant senior official of an organization or institution. In the case of a media participant, these terms could refer to a journalist's senior editor or the chair of the board of a media enterprise. In the case of a business organization, these terms might be the appropriate senior reporting officer, the Chief Executive Officer, or the chair of the board of directors. What is relevant is that most individuals with an institutional position who participate in multistakeholder governance arrangements do so not on their own personal or professional account, but as someone with an organizational boss.

Types of multistakeholder governance groups

Multistakeholder governance groups tend to fall into three different categories dependent on the locus of their activity and the governance gaps they are designed to address.

Policy-oriented multistakeholder governance groups

The first of these functional categories are multistakeholder governance structures whose founding premise is to address an international policy issue. These policy-oriented MSGs tend to be created from the conjuncture of two factors: an unwillingness of governments or an intergovernmental organization to tackle a policy matter and a strong self-interest of major global actors that some policy intervention is absolutely necessary. Consequently, most policy-oriented MSGs are intentionally convened independent of the multilateral system. For example, the World Economic Forum's Network of Global Future Councils has a separate group on The Future of International Governance, Public-Private Cooperation & Sustainable Development. According to this group's terms of reference, which include an explicit distancing from the multilateral system, it expects to:

> promote, syndicate and discuss latest trends and technologies and solutions at the nexus of public-private cooperation and sustainable development delivery against the 2030 Agenda. This includes: – The role of multi-stakeholder partnerships to address the global challenges of sustainable development – The role of international organizations in global decision-making – Transnational expert networks providing an alternative to intergovernmental coordination.
>
> (WEF n.d.)

Table 1.2 has other examples of policy-oriented MSGs created to close a global or regional governance gap.

Some of these policy-oriented MSGs may establish a pro forma connection with the multilateral system. After a policy-oriented MSG establishes its direction in a specific area, governments associated with the MSG may bring this initiative to the intergovernmental system for its endorsement or acceptance. This process was followed by the multistakeholder Kimberly Process Certification Scheme on conflict diamonds (Kimberly Process Certification Scheme n.d.). While selected African governments, three CSOs, and the world diamond industry developed their plan to prevent diamonds from conflict areas reaching the international market, the UN system was asked to explicitly defer potential actions and await the outcome of this autonomously created multistakeholder body. After the plan was announced, the General Assembly endorsed the proposals from the Kimberly Process Certification Scheme and in so doing granted international leadership to that multistakeholder body.

Product and process-oriented (standard-setting) multistakeholder groups

The second functional category of multistakeholder governance structures are organizations set up to create criteria for products and processes in international trade and to provide a platform where potentially conflicting views between commercial participants in a given market can be reconciled.

For many decades the international standard-setting process for technologies and products was led by the multistakeholder International Organization for Standardization (ISO) (see Chapter 3 for further information on

Table 1.2 Examples of global policy-oriented multistakeholder groups

Multistakeholder group	Policy arena	Self-description of structure
World Commission on Dams	Review of plans, construction records, operation and maintenance of dams	A dialogue between civil society, governments, affected local communities, scientists, financial institutions, and the private sector to assess alternative options for meeting water and energy needs. Recommendations of the report have been incorporated into national development policies and public dialogue processes.
Global Agenda Council on the Arctic, World Economic Forum	Investment in the Arctic region with a focus on environmental protection	Developed the Arctic Investment Protocol: six investment objectives, challenges and opportunities for sustainable development, good business practices, and effective resource management in the region. Scientific and environmental researchers, the Arctic Business Council, and political actors influenced the drafting of the Protocol with the intention to assist governments and businesses to responsibly invest in the region.
Kimberley Process Certification Scheme	Prevent worldwide trade of conflict diamonds	A binding agreement with sophisticated standards for participants with the elimination of trading conflict diamonds as the highest priority. Participants are required to adapt national policies, government bodies, and import/export controls to KPCS requirements, enable transparent trade processes, limit trade activities only with other participants, and certify shipments as conflict-free.
Renewable Policy Network for the 21st Century	Renewable energy	Global renewable energy policy multistakeholder network that connects governments, NGOs, research and academic institutions, and industry to facilitate knowledge exchange, policy development, and joint action toward a rapid global transition to renewable energy.

Table 1.2 Continued

Multistakeholder group	Policy arena	Self-description of structure
Global Partnership for Oceans	Sustainable ocean investment	A blue ribbon panel of 21 global experts from 16 counties representing the private sector, non-profit organizations, academia and multi-lateral institutions that provided recommendations for prioritizing and implementing sustainable ocean investment.

Sources in order cited: International Rivers n.d.; The Polar Connection 2016; Kimberly Process Certification Scheme n.d.; REN21 n.d.; World Bank 2015.

the governance of the ISO). This category of MSG has two sub-categories. The first sub-category is for those MSGs that seek to incorporate ethical, environmental, or developmental product or process criteria in international trade. Their objective is to prod purchasers to make more socially aware purchasing decisions and to support a sufficiently robust market following socially oriented criteria that producers, manufacturers, and retailers correspondingly also find the criteria beneficial in their business activities.

The proliferation of these non-state and non-ISO standard-setting bodies has been so extensive that they now have their own specialized trade association, the International Social and Environmental Accreditation and Labelling Alliance (ISEAL) to support their certification, verification, and internal organizational requirements. While these independent standard-setting multistakeholder bodies engage some TNCs, exporting countries, and large domestic purchasers in a market, they face challenges from other powerful actors (i.e., other TNCs, other exporting countries, and other large purchasers) who are quite comfortable maintaining the business-as-usual market system with its harmful environmental, social, and economic aspects. In other words, multistakeholder standard-setting groups have no effective sanctioning power over the parts of their market that elect not to follow the lead of the voluntary standard-setting body.

In this area, the international governance gap is the political and economic space created by non-action of the multilateral system. For example, a number of intergovernmental organizations focus in whole or in part on wood products and sustainable development – such as the International Tropical Timber Organization, the Food and Agriculture Organization (FAO), the United Nations Conference on Trade and Development (UNCTAD), or the United Nations Forum on Forests. Nevertheless, these organizations have simply avoided any meaningful decision-making on what constitutes sustainable forestry practices. This has opened up the

20 *Multilateralism and multistakeholderism*

political space for a collection of concerned foresters, tree companies, biodiversity experts, wood retailers, and tree workers associations to establish independent bodies such as the Forest Stewardship Council. Bernstein and Cashore (2007) see these product-oriented MSG systems as "deliberative and adaptive governance institutions designed to embed social and environmental norms in the global marketplace that derive authority directly from interested audiences, including those they seek to regulate, not from sovereign states."

Table 1.3 has examples of other international product and process-oriented MSGs.

Table 1.3 Examples of environmental and social standard-setting multistakeholder groups

Multistakeholder group	Economic-social sector	Self-description of activity
International Seafood Sustainability Foundation	Sustainable global tuna fisheries	To undertake and facilitate science-based initiatives for the long-term conservation and sustainable use of global tuna stocks, reducing bycatch and promoting tuna ecosystem health.
Initiative for Responsible Mining Assurance	Responsible mining assurance system	To establish a multistakeholder and independently verified responsible mining assurance system that improves social and environmental performance.
Global Sustainable Tourism Council	Sustainable tourism practices	Develops international standards; serves as the accreditation body for sustainability in travel and tourism making destinations sustainable; promotes market access and increases knowledge.
International Council of Toy Industries (ICTI) Care	Ethical supply chain program for the global toy industry	Works with thousands of brands, retailers, suppliers, NGOs and other civil society groups to monitor, manage, and fix social sustainability issues in the toy industry supply chain across the world and to protect and improve labor standards.
Better Cotton Initiative	Sustainable way of growing cotton	Generating market demand for Better Cotton, and sharing information and knowledge to enable continuous improvement on everybody's part.

Sources in order cited: ISSF, n.d.; IRMA n.d.; GSTC 2017; ICTI CARE n.d.; BCI, n.d.

Another sub-category of standard-setting MSGs are those MSGs whose primary purpose is to convene the leading firms in a given market for new and high-impact technologies in order to build a consensus on how these new technologies can function across national boundaries without the engagement of the ISO, while providing a platform in which to reconcile the views of social justice civil society organizations as well as academic and government bodies on the best route forward. This second sub-category is generally based on the governance of rapidly evolving and complex technologies which require a high level of invested science and capital and have currently a low level of government established standards. An example of this sub-category is ICANN – the Internet Corporation for Assigned Names and Numbers – and the governance of the internet. Table 1.4 has additional background on this group of standard-setting multi-stakeholder bodies.

This second sub-category of standard-setting multistakeholder organizations is not designed to respond to any existing governance gap but rather to explicitly distance itself from the role of government and the multilateral system in its governance. In the case of internet governance, the drive for a multistakeholder governance system was to avoid working with the follow-up to the Internet Governance Forum created by the World Summit on the Information Society and the International Telecommunication Union (ITU). For tens of decades, the ITU has successfully governed the technology of telephones (e.g., telephone switching stations and designation of country codes) and the technology and economics of postal services (e.g., standardization of prices for international services and guarantees for free speech in delivery of postal documents). The World Summit on the Information Society was open to all governments and a wide range of internet-connected constituencies as non-state participants. For those driving the creation of ICANN, the interest was to create an autonomous multistakeholder political space away from both the ITU and governments. As a result of the complex forces in its history and its crucial economic role, internet governance is probably the multistakeholder segment with the most robust debate on governance.

In a similar context, WEF's report on oceans and biodiversity observed:

> ... Harnessing [new] opportunities and proactively managing these risks will require a transformation of the "enabling environment," namely the governance frameworks and policy protocols, investment and financing models, the prevailing incentives for technology development, and the nature of societal engagement. This transformation will not happen automatically. It will require proactive collaboration between policymakers, scientists, civil society, technology champions and investors.
>
> (WEF 2017: 3)

Table 1.4 Examples of high-impact technology standard-setting multistakeholder groups

Multistakeholder group	Economic-social sector	Self-description of activity
ICANN	Internet-related governance	ICANN's vision is that of an independent, global organization trusted worldwide to coordinate the global internet's systems of unique identifiers to support a single, open, globally interoperable internet. ICANN builds trust through serving the public interest, and incorporating the transparent and effective cooperation among stakeholders worldwide to facilitate its coordination role.
The FramingNano Project	Nanotechnology-related governance	The objective of FramingNano is to support the establishment of a multistakeholder dialogue on NS&T (nanotechnology, science and technology) regulation and governance involving the scientific, institutional and industrial communities as well as the broader public. The objective of the project is to articulate consensus and absence of consensus between the various stakeholders, … and foster the development of a shared frame of knowledge, objectives and actions leading to constructive and practicable regulatory solutions (governance plan) for the responsible development of NS&T at the European level (and beyond).
Global Partnership for Business and Biodiversity	Biodiversity-related governance	The Conference of Parties to the Biodiversity Convention calls upon businesses to continue liaising with national governments, civil society organizations, academia and other stakeholders to formulate relevant actions for biodiversity conservation.
Carnegie Climate Geoengineering Governance Initiative	Geoengineering climate adaptation technologies	[Seeks] to catalyze the creation of effective governance for climate geoengineering technologies by shifting the conversation from the scientific and research community to the global policy-making arena, and by encouraging a broader, society-wide discussion about the risks, potential benefits, ethical and governance challenges raised by climate geoengineering.

Sources in order cited: ICANN 2013; Mantovani et al. 2009; von Schomberg and Davies 2010; Convention on Biological Diversity 2012; C2G2 n.d.

A significant difference between the two sub-categories of standard-setting MSGs is the degree of emphasis each provides to the two shared functions. The first sub-category places a higher goal on introducing value-based criteria into an international market while acting to reconcile the differences between types of business sectors involved in a given market. The second sub-category reverses the attention to these goals. The primary goal of these MSGs is to reconcile competing commercial interests in a newly developing technological market while providing a platform for multiple actors concerned with social justice matters to engage in the process. Because of this difference in emphasis, the first sub-category is subsequently referred to as environmental and social standard-setting MSGs while the second sub-category is referred to as high-impact technology standard-setting MSGs.

Project-oriented multistakeholder groups

The third functional category, and most-likely the largest number of independent multistakeholder governance groups, are those which take on a specific global or local task that reasonably one might have expected, say twenty-five years ago, would have been considered a responsibility of government or the multilateral system. As with the standard-setting category, these project-oriented MSGs have two sub-categories.

The first sub-category is at the international level. These international project-oriented groups fill a governance implementation gap created by the multilateral system itself. This governance gap may be self-declared, as when the UN system acknowledges that it lacks the managerial and financial capacity to implement its own declared goals. It can also arise when the multilateral system acknowledges a problem area but only issues a general statement or resolution, leaving effective responses to other international actors. As these policy MSGs are independent of the intergovernmental system, they can – and do – reformulate intergovernmental goals in often subtle ways into goals that are more aligned with the self-interest of the MSGs participants. Table 1.5 has examples of global project-oriented MSGs.

The second sub-category are those task-focused MSGs largely at the national level where TNCs perceive a market opportunity involving an under-met public need and where the relevant government authority does not have – or does not perceive that it has – the capacity to act. This sub-category of task-focused MSGs are generally called public-private partnerships (PPPs). Examples include PPPs to redesign a local drinking water system, develop a series of health clinics for local workers, or stabilize the biodiversity in a given area. As these infrastructure projects tend to involve a significant commitment of capital, a long duration, and a complex income stream, they tend to be memorialized in formal legal agreements.

Table 1.5 Examples of global project-oriented multistakeholder groups

Multistakeholder group	Project self-description
Alliance for Water Stewardship	A global membership-based collaboration to address the changing nature of water-related challenges. Promotes sustainable water management.
Roll Back Malaria	A global platform for coordinated action against malaria. It mobilizes for action and resources and forges consensus among members.
Accord on Fire and Building Safety in Bangladesh	A five-year independent, legally binding agreement between global brands and retailers and trade unions designed to build a safe and healthy Bangladeshi Ready-Made Garment industry.
Global Alliance for Improved Nutrition	Mobilizes public-private partnerships and provides financial and technical support to deliver nutritious foods to those people most at risk of malnutrition.
Toilet Board Coalition	A business platform enabling private sector engagement; connecting large and small companies; and ensuring close collaboration between private, public and non-profit sectors with the common goal to accelerate the business of sanitation for all.
The Global Polio Eradication Initiative	The goal is to complete the eradication and containment of all wild, vaccine-related and Sabin polio viruses, such that no child ever again suffers paralytic poliomyelitis.
The Global Fund to Fight AIDs, Tuberculosis and Malaria	A partnership organization designed to accelerate the end of AIDS, tuberculosis and malaria as epidemics.
Sustainable Energy for All	Sustainable Energy for All empowers leaders to broker partnerships and unlock finance to achieve universal access to sustainable energy.

Sources in order cited: Alliance for Water Stewardship n.d.; RBM n.d.; Accord on Fire and Building Safety in Bangladesh n.d.; GAIN n.d.; UN Foundation Global Alliance for Clean Cookstoves n.d.; Toilet Board Coalition n.d.; Polio Global Eradication Initiative n.d.; The Global Fund 2017; Sustainable Energy for All n.d.

A PPP usually involves a combination of government offices from national authorities, to provincial authorities, to municipal authorities. As most large infrastructure projects cross over a number of domestic boundaries, there can be multiple provincial and multiple municipal authorities in any given PPP. In addition, the "public" side can also include a number of local community organizations, international CSOs, international experts, and representatives from national environmental and social NGOs. On the private side, a PPP can include not only the lead international investor, but also its domestic business partners, multilateral banks, and domestic financing organizations.[7] While the ambiguity surrounding the "public" part of the acronym makes "PPP" an inaccurate phrase, it has gained wide acceptance as a term of art.

These initiatives gain traction from the relative political weakness of a nation-state and its local authorities which are responding to the self-interest of dominant actors in a given territory to tackle a problem and generate a business profit. As these project-oriented MSGs are created to fix a perceived governance gap, the approach they take to a project often acts to re-define the social and political landscape around the project area.

These three different forms of MSGs have evolved along separate paths. In recent years, these paths have merged to become the institutional foundation for multistakeholderism. Chapter 2 describes the separate paths and the routes they have taken to converge and gain public legitimacy as a candidate for the next form of global governance. Because of the multiple tracks in the evolution of multistakeholderism, no intergovernmental or public vote is necessary for a multistakeholder governance system to supplant multilateralism as the leading global governance institution.

Notes

1 The "UN system" refers to the UN and all the intergovernmental specialized agencies, programs, and offices. For a listing of the organizational members of the UN system, see www.unsceb.org/directory. Note that the WTO and the Basel institutions remain outside the UN system but that the head of WTO participates in UN system coordination meetings.
2 The exception here being the ability of states to use military power to secure natural resources and access to markets, and trade agreements to open markets and protect patents.
3 The exceptions are rivers, lakes, and other land-bounded water bodies.
4 Exceptions to this include the "Commission of Experts on Reforms of the International Financial and Monetary System" led by Miguel d'Escoto Brockmann, President of the General Assembly, and Joseph Stiglitz of Columbia University (Stiglitz 2010).
5 See Chapter 3 for further background on the Westphalian system.
6 Stakeholders that are said to represent an institution such as a UN agency, a government department, or a funding body are in a different category. Their roles in MSGs are explained in Chapters 3 and 4.
7 Brinkerhoff and Brinkerhoff (2011: 31) explain:

> Practitioners and scholars have used the term "partnership" to describe just about any type of collaboration between state and non-state actors. Also the vast and growing literature on public–private partnerships suffers from conceptual confusion, competing definitions, disparate research traditions, and a normative and value-laden agenda of promoting partnerships. This state of conceptual vagueness has led some scholars to describe the term partnership as "conceptually empty and merely politically expedient."

References

Accord on Fire and Building Safety in Bangladesh. n.d. "About the Accord." Accessed March 7, 2018. Available from http://bangladeshaccord.org/about/.

Alliance for Water Stewardship. n.d. "Join the Alliance for Water Stewardship." Accessed March 7, 2018. Available from http://a4ws.org/get-involved/join/.

Avant, Deborah D., Martha Finnemore, and Susan K. Sell. 2010. *Who Governs the Globe?* Cambridge: Cambridge University Press.

BCI. n.d. "Who we are." Accessed March 7, 2018. Available from https://bettercotton.org/about-bci/who-we-are/.

Bernstein, Steven, and Benjamin Cashore. 2007. "Can non-state global governance be legitimate? An analytical framework." *Regulation & Governance* 1, no. 4: 347–371.

Brinkerhoff, Derick W., and Jennifer M. Brinkerhoff. 2011. "Public-private partnerships: Perspectives on purposes, publicness, and good governance." *Public Administration and Development* 31, no. 1: 2–14.

C2G2. n.d. "C2G2 Mission." Accessed March 7, 2018. Available from www.c2g2.net/c2g2-mission/.

Convention on Biological Diversity. 2012. *Decision Adopted by the Conference of the Parties to the Convention on Biological Diversity at its Eleventh Meeting.* Hyderabad, India, UNEP/CBD/COP/DEC/XI/7 (October 8–19, 2012; adopted December 5, 2012). Available from www.cbd.int/doc/decisions/cop-11/cop-11-dec-07-en.pdf.

FAO Committee on World Food Security. n.d. "CFS Structure." Accessed July 1, 2017. Available from www.fao.org/cfs/home/about/structure/en/.

GSTC. 2017. "What is the GSTC?" Last modified August 24, 2017. Available from www.gstcouncil.org/about/about-us/.

ICANN. 2013. "Strategic Planning." Last modified October 10, 2013. Available from www.icann.org/resources/pages/strategic-engagement-2013-10-10-en.

ICTI CARE. n.d. "About ICTI CARE." Accessed March 7, 2018. Available from http://pastbackup.com/e/content/cat_page.asp?cat_id=285.

International Rivers. n.d. "The World Commission on Dams." Accessed July 1, 2017. Available from www.internationalrivers.org/campaigns/the-world-commission-on-dams.

IRMA. n.d. "About IRMA." Accessed December 7, 2017. Available from www.responsiblemining.net/about-irma/.

ISSF. n.d. "About." Accessed December 7, 2017. Available from https://iss-foundation.org/who-we-are/about/.

Kimberly Process Certification Scheme. n.d. "About." Accessed July 1, 2017. Available from www.kimberleyprocess.com/en/about/.

Mantovani, Elvio, Andrew Porcari, Christoph Meili, and Markus Widmer. 2009. "FramingNano Project: A multistakeholder dialogue platform framing the responsible development of Nanosciences & Nanotechnologies." Rome: Framing Nano Project, Report prepared by AIRI/Nanotec IT, The Innovation Society.

Polio Global Eradication Initiative. n.d. "Our Mission." Accessed March 3, 2018. Available from http://polioeradication.org/who-we-are/our-mission/.

Potts, Andy. 2016. "Internet Governance: We the Networks." *The Economist*, March 5, 2016. Available from www.economist.com/news/international/21693922-organisation-runs-internet-address-book-about-declare-independence-we.

RBM. n.d. "About RBM." Accessed March 7, 2018. Available from https://rollbackmalaria.com/about-rbm/.
REN21. n.d. "About us." Accessed July 1, 2017. Available from www.ren21.net/about-ren21/about-us/.
Stiglitz, Joseph E and Members of the UN Commission of Financial Experts. 2010. "The Stiglitz Report: Reforming the International Monetary and Financial Systems in the Wake of the Global Crisis". New York: New Press.
Sustainable Energy for All. n.d. "Our Mission." Accessed March 7, 2018. Available from www.seforall.org/our-work.
The Global Fund. 2017. "Global Fund Overview." Last modified November 17, 2017. Available from www.theglobalfund.org/en/overview/.
The Polar Connection. 2016. "World Economic Forum Launches Arctic Investment Protocol." Accessed August 24, 2016. Available from http://polarconnection.org/arctic-investment-protocol-december-2015/.
Toilet Board Coalition. n.d. "Who We Are." Accessed March 7, 2018. Available from www.toiletboard.org/about-the-tbc.
UN. n.d. "High-Level Political Forum on Sustainable Development." Accessed July 1, 2017. Available from https://sustainabledevelopment.un.org/hlpf.
UN Foundation Global Alliance for Clean Cookstoves. n.d. "About." Accessed March 7, 2018. Available from http://cleancookstoves.org/about/.
United Nations Forum on Forests. n.d. "Multi-Stakeholder Dialogue." Accessed July 1, 2017. Available from www.un.org/esa/forests/major-groups/multi-stakeholder-dialogue/index.html.
von Schomberg, R. and S. Davies. 2010. "Understanding Public Debate on Nanotechnologies: Options for Framing Public Policy." Luxembourg: Publication Office of the European Union.
WEF. n.d. Global Future Councils on the Future of International Governance, Public-Private Cooperation & Sustainable Development. Accessed April 4, 2018. Available from www.weforum.org/communities/the-future-of-international-governance-public-private-cooperation.
WEF. 2010. "Global Redesign: Strengthening International Cooperation in a More Interdependent World." Geneva: World Economic Forum.
WEF. 2017. "Harnessing the Fourth Industrial Revolution for Oceans. Geneva: World Economic Forum in collaboration with PwC and Stanford Woods Institute for the Environment." Geneva: World Economic Forum.
World Bank. 2015. "Global Partnership for Oceans (GPO)." Last modified July 1, 2015. Available from www.worldbank.org/en/topic/environment/brief/global-partnership-for-oceans-gpo.

2 How did we get here?
A convergence of multiple trends

Villages and towns did not disappear with the evolution of counties, provinces, and states; they just lost a good deal of their political clout. As counties, provinces, and states further consolidated into kingdoms and nations, lower-level units lost considerable power to their senior units. If the age of multistakeholderism is the next form of global governance, multilateralism and regionalism will continue to exist, but in a politically weaker state.

Indicative of this shift is the extent that the nation-state governments and public authorities have been moved – and have moved themselves – out of the driver seat when it comes to making global governance decisions. They have often accepted their new secondary or marginal roles, as if this is the new normal. The leaders in this new form of global governance are an amalgamation of designated "stakeholders," collectively known as "multistakeholders." This terminology was not previously part of the lexicon of international relations but it has been powerfully elevated to a new status. There has been, however, no evaluation of multistakeholderism or even a clear functional definition of this form of global governance. In effect, the proliferation of multistakeholder governance arrangements, each with its own raison d'être, has created experimental platforms for testing different modes of multistakeholder governance.

This chapter explores twelve political and economic developments that have created the international political space for these experiments. The first four of these political realities are derived from institutional failures – or the perception of institutional failures – to manage current macro-economic, social, and ecological global crises. The next four reflect the fundamental transition over the past fifty years in the relationship between the UN system, TNCs and CSOs, respectively. This includes changes in how certain TNCs and CSOs perceive members of the other camp and how TNCs and globally powerful elites have come to recognize the need for some new quasi-state function at the international level. The last four tracks exemplify how different international forces have come to accept that multistakeholder governance has the potential to be the next phase of global governance.

Macro political-economic factors

Proliferation of major unresolved international crises

A series of major international crises have prompted the recognition by members of the international community that the current combination of nation-states, regional organizations, and multilateralism cannot manage the social and economic consequences of globalization or protect the global ecological system (ISS 2010: 11).

Across the globe, major crises keep appearing unexpectedly. On the financial side, the Latin American debt crisis (early 1980s), Asian financial crisis (1998), and the Global Recession (2008/2009) appeared to come out of nowhere. The institutions assigned global monetary and financial responsibility were not able to forewarn the world of these crises. On the environmental side, global climate change, coral reef whiting, and transboundary air and water pollution have seen only tepid governmental and intergovernmental responses. None of the official UN system climate interventions have significantly slowed down the rate of increase of greenhouse gases in the atmosphere. No government or international agency has stepped forward to take responsibility for handling domestic toxins that have migrated to the Arctic Circle or international waters.

Regarding social and human affairs, the UN system hosted a series of global conferences in the 1990s culminating in the Millennium Development Goals (MDGs – early 2000s) and the Sustainable Development Goals (SDGs – 2015), while the overall level of global inequality has increased sharply. On the peace and security front, the world has endured major military interventions by the US, Russia, and their allies in Iraq, Libya, Syria, Yemen, and Afghanistan, Russian interventions in Crimea and the Ukraine, and long-standing regional conflicts in Central Africa (Congo), Israel/Palestine, and elsewhere without any effective counter-weight from the existing governance organizations. Looking at global health management, the world's inadequate response to SARS and other pandemics has engendered a global health nervousness. Simultaneously, the unanticipated sharp growth in involuntary migration has resulted in a disconcertingly high number of migrant deaths.

What these crises have in common is that each of them in its own way was unexpected, and subsequently the multilateral system responded with an inadequate patchwork of actions. The financial crisis created the Financial Stability Board; the climate crisis created the voluntary Paris Agreement (UNFCCC 2017); humanitarian crises have created resolutions without the necessary commitment of resources; the global health crisis has led to a weakened World Health Organization (WHO); the involuntary immigration crisis has produced a number of ad hoc human rights organizations and the overall militarization of the management of migration (International Federation for Human Rights 2016); and the world has come to expect that the Security Council cannot truly maintain peace.

The cumulative impact of these unresolved global crises has led to a sentiment that the international community must try something different in global governance. In this sense, multistakeholder governance and its accompanying collection of powerful actors has drawn support as a candidate system that just may be able to address these unresolved global crises.

Perception of multilateralism as a dysfunctional system

With each new crisis, the existing UN system and other components of the global governance system appear overwhelmed. Each global crisis is accompanied by public critiques regarding the failure of international institutions. The cumulative effect is that pressure has grown to ask other institutions – almost any other institution – to play a role in preventing these unexpected events and to deal with the potentially severe consequences.

In the 1960s and 1970s, the UN and Security Council in particular were severely constrained by the Cold War and by North–South inter-regional battles. By the 1980s, however, factions in the US and elsewhere were advancing critiques about the functional failures of the UN, generating fears of black helicopters taking over a country. This community developed the meme that the UN wanted to militarily and economically rule the world, taking power away from nation-states.

The 1980s and early 1990s saw a series of globally important conferences focused on setting new global directions for the role of women, housing, poverty, the environment, population and development. The underlying assumption behind these conferences was that a multi-sector approach to reducing poverty and inequality would ultimately result in a significant impact backed by the commitment of the international community. In these conferences of the 90s, as they are called, the UN system led in helping to define and re-define global public needs, global public goods and the global commons. This conceptual leadership and policy development, however, was undermined by national government decisions in parallel to freeze the budget resources of the UN and its sister organizations. No-growth budgets – or even net-negative budgets – have for over a quarter of a century stymied implementation of many of the aspirations expressed by these international conferences. As OECD member states understood the contradiction between the hosting of global conferences on pressing global needs and their own decisions not to supplement international funding to address these needs, they opted instead to discourage further meetings on the management of global social, economic, and environmental crisis, pleading "no-new-conferences and no-new-organizations."[1]

By the mid-1990s, several economic and functional critiques of the UN system (absent the helicopters) had moved into the mainstream. Notably, there was an Iraqi corruption investigation that over-publicized minor improper transactions, a US suspension of dues payments to UNESCO and the UN as they did not deliver what the US administration wanted, and failed efforts to weaken the veto and to introduce new countries as permanent members of the Security Council. Nevertheless, most of these investigations, financial threats, and reform efforts produced no fundamental shift by member states in regard to how they chose to operate inside or outside the UN system.[2] Irrespective of the specific accuracy of each claim, the over-arching public media message was that the United Nations system was not the platform for organizing a truly efficient, obligatory, low-cost, and fully accountable solution to global or regional problems. Cumulatively, a public feeling developed that the United Nations system could not deliver.

Subsequently, by the turn of the millennium, it was clear that increases in core UN system funding was not going to shift significantly in response to election changes in any of the major donor countries. It was also clear that other governments were not prepared to take over the financial lead in underwriting the international system.

To complicate matters, in the public eye, governments and the media portray the United Nations, the specialized agencies, the World Bank, and the IMF as one institution. This is a convenient message for governments to nurture when they have complaints about the international system. In practice and in law, however, this one-institution image is incorrect on two grounds, each of which acts to expose a structural contradiction in multilateral governance.

By design, the UN system is comprised of over thirty separate organizations, each with its own mandate, constitutional document, governing body, financial arrangements, and secretariat. The General Assembly of the UN has no legal authority to oversee or instruct the governing bodies of the International Monetary Fund (IMF), the WHO, the FAO or any of the other specialized international governing bodies. This institutional fragmentation evolved as a series of choices by governments from WWII onwards to keep the organizations independent of each other and to restrict their scope of activity. As more and more contemporary international issues are cross-cutting in their origins and thus require a cross-sectorial response to be effective, the operational consequences of the designed fragmentation have become clearer and clearer. Yet there is little government or UN system enthusiasm for merging institutions or providing a common governance super-structure.

The second difficulty with the one-institution image is one of terminology. For the UN and most parts of the UN system, the public name of the intergovernmental body and its support staff is the same. When the public hears "the United Nations," it is not clear if the reference is to the organizational staff of the body, known as the secretariat, or the governments which set policy and provide directions to the secretariat. When one hears that the FAO announced a policy direction, it is ambiguous if the declaration was from the intergovernmental body (did governments make that policy statement?) or from its secretariat (did the head of staff just release the results of a research study?). This ambiguity today means that the public does not understand who is accountable for any badly implemented plan. As a whole, however, the UN system is an association of governments that chooses to – or not to – use the capacities of the international system to address global issues. When governments are reluctant to collectively address a global crisis, the UN can be portrayed as a dysfunctional scapegoat.

This degree of public frustration has led to suggestions to look elsewhere for an effective or efficient organization to deal with international or regional problems. Multistakeholder arrangements – with or without the UN system – have thus become a governance candidate by default. Intergovernmental bodies and their secretariats can be involved but only as one player in these new arrangements.

Weakening of the nation-states' ability to manage globalization and to protect the global ecosystem

Part of the operational and conceptual weakness of the multilateralism system follows from fundamental changes in the domestic economic management of the OECD countries. During the Thatcher and Reagan administrations of the 1980s, the UK and the USA began a two-fold process to shift the balance of power between the nation-state and their domestic economies. Arguing persuasively that the state should allow the market to make more social, ecological, and economic decisions, they professed that the way to facilitate this transfer of authority from the public domain to the private sector was through economic deregulation. This meant that government agencies charged with protecting public health, worker safety, the domestic ecological systems, and other public concerns should now weaken formal regulations, look for ways to transfer authority to less powerful sub-national bodies, and include in their cost-benefit calculations the likely costs to the private sector. These political economic-social changes undertaken inside OECD countries fundamentally affected governance realities at the international level.

At the same time, domestic political, social, and economic decisions by the Russian, Chinese, Indian and other governments affected approaches to international economic, social, and environmental governance. These governments began aggressively imposing domestic market austerity, deregulating their economies, and courting inward TNC investment, in part driven by their debt burdens and their currency volatility and in part pushed by the IMF and the World Bank. Due to these domestic realities, these governments shifted away from intervening in global markets, even when they knew doing so contributed to their domestic difficulties.

Cumulatively, these policy changes created a barrier to international engagement with the private sector except on a non-regulatory, voluntary basis.

Any major effort to address global climate change, such as the 1997 Kyoto Protocol (UNFCCC n.d.) and the 2017 Paris climate accord (UNFCCC 2017), had their content based on market interventions, self-regulation, and volunteerism. In the case of the global economy, the message from foreign affairs spokespersons at the UN was first and foremost that the UN should not even debate formulating intergovernmental positions on trade, monetary, macro-economic policy or specific economic markets. At the ideological level, the adulation of global public-private partnerships heightened, with them being presented as intrinsically positive and the most appropriate way to tackle globally expensive challenges. The drive toward domestic deregulation combined with its impact on foreign affairs departments meant that intergovernmental bodies stepped back from even attempting to set rules for globalization or to take any potentially obligatory joint actions to protect the planet.

Out of this political vacuum has emerged an expanded search for new partners to replace state functions at the international level. Not all of the new potential partners favor democracy.

The rise of authoritarianism invites an appeal to a socially-wider decision-making system

The growth of authoritarianism – the concentration of economic power in fewer and fewer hands, the greater tolerance for explicit racism, the hostility of nation-states against immigrants, and the electoral advances of right-wing parties – all create a foreboding image for the future. The uptick in authoritarianism is most noticeable in the OECD countries, but it is a global phenomenon stretching from the Philippines to Turkey, to Venezuela, to Eastern Europe (TNI 2017). The concentration of wealth in the hands of the 0.1 percent discourages expectations of meaningful upward mobility and increases skepticism about the legitimacy of existing international political processes. Global civil rights movements have watched as one minority after the other is singled out as socially unacceptable partners in society, thus being further marginalized from the political process. Involuntary migration within and between countries is another form of extreme marginalization. The expansion of the right within the democratic nation-states has resulted in attacks on key social groups in a country as not worthy of participating in national democracies, let alone global ones.

In this context, another form of governance has extended a welcoming hand. It offers non-state actors, some of whom have seen their communities unexpectedly attacked in recent decades, a full seat at the global governance table. Multistakeholderism looks like a meaningful counterweight against the full speed expansion of authoritarianism. It asserts that every group with a stake in an issue should be involved, not excluded, from addressing the issue. It says that ethnic diversity, gender diversity, cultural diversity are all good things and that individuals and organizations from these communities should be elevated into the global governance conversation.

In the context of the growth of authoritarianism and its related exclusionary forces, multistakeholderism can sound like a good way forward.

Structural transformations

In parallel with these political-economic factors, the dynamic between the UN system, its member governments, the international business community, and the non-profit sector has been changing, sometimes in a long, slowly drawn out process and sometimes very abruptly. These transformations have shifted the landscape of global governance in ways that were unexpected even ten years before they happened.

Transformation of the relationship between TNCs and the UN system

From the end of WWII until the 1960s, multinational corporations largely ignored the UN system as relatively immaterial to their global business strategy. From their own perspective, governments similarly did not see the private sector as relevant in global governance, and corporations, unlike NGOs, were not even mentioned in the UN Charter. By the early 2000s, however, this status of disengagement had significantly shifted. Today, corporate CEOs happily meet the UN's Secretary-General, and intergovernmental bodies send letters of invitation to TNCs inviting them to participate in developing policies and implementing UN system projects.

The transformation of the relationship between TNCs and the UN system occurred through an uneven process.

In the 1970s, ITT, a major investor in the Chilean mining sector, was actively involved in overthrowing the elected government of President Salvador Allende. After this became public knowledge in Latin America, the G77 approached the Secretary-General to establish a UN program focusing on transnational corporations (Hamdani and Ruffing 2015). Some governments saw a role for the UN in establishing a code of conduct for TNCs to level the playing field in developing countries. At the same time, TNC executives saw a role for the UN in dampening the anti-TNC ethos that was growing in developing countries. Senior corporate executives participated in a high-level panel of experts in recommending the establishment of the Commission on Transnational Corporations with a standing secretariat, the UN Centre on Transnational Corporations (UNCTC). However, most other firms and business trade associations saw the involvement of the UN system regarding issues relating to TNCs as a danger. In their minds, governments and the UN could become potential challengers to their operational interests in an unregulated international market.

The Commission on Transnational Corporations and its Secretariat were given three tasks: (1) to formulate a code of conduct; (2) to encourage foreign direct investment while minimizing the negative consequences of foreign direct investment; and (3) to assist developing countries in their negotiations with TNCs (ECOSOC 1974). The initial goodwill toward the work of this organization diminished as the Commission and UNCTC faced increasing opposition from the TNC community and OECD governments, particularly considering UNCTC's support for divestment from South Africa, recommendations on environmental and social standards for TNCs, and the provision of clear legal and economic advice to countries negotiating with major firms. In competition with the new work on TNCs at the UN, the OECD began its own effort to formulate global policy on TNCs (OECD 2008: 5) and the International Chamber of Commerce (ICC) created a separate corporate-led body to coordinate business responses on environmental matters.

While these debates were going on through the mid-1980s, specialized agencies and UN programs and funds, led by FAO's Industry Cooperation Program (FAO 2017) and UNDP's Growing Inclusive Markets Initiative (UNDP 2008), began opening dedicated business windows in their organizations to reach out to TNCs to establish partnerships between the UN and the private sector. Eventually, almost all UN specialized agencies and subsidiary bodies established dedicated offices to partner with the corporate sector. As part of this outreach by the UN system to TNCs, the World Bank established its International Finance Corporation to support project-based "public-private partnerships" with international businesses.

The preparations for the June 1992 Rio Conference on Environment and Development marked a change in the relationship between the international corporate sector and the UN. Under the leadership of the Secretary-General of the Conference, Maurice Strong, TNCs were welcomed to actively participate in the conference. Some innovative CEOs saw this as opportunity to create the Business Council for Sustainable Development.[3] This elevated corporate engagement with the UN system and sustainable development from the Vice-President level at the ICC to the CEO level, replacing the ICC as the lead corporate spokes-organization on these matters. With Strong's encouragement, TNCs began to make direct financial contributions to the UN. In turn, the Rio Conference recommendations and the UN General Assembly began including language explicitly welcoming TNCs to carry out UN-adopted policy goals.

At the same time, the Commission and the Centre were then under political pressure from the right-of-center forces in the US. Following the Rio Conference, Secretary-General Boutros Boutros Ghali closed the Centre and transferred some of its functions to UNCTAD. In the transfer to UNCTAD, two major changes were made to the scope of its work. The

36 *A convergence of multiple trends*

first original task – a call for a code of conduct – was dropped from the terms of reference. The second task – the instruction to encourage the growth of foreign direct investment (FDI) while minimizing the negative consequences – had its entire last phrase deleted.

Seven years later in 1999, Secretary-General Kofi Annan announced on the margin of the World Economic Forum that he intended to set up a Global Compact with multinational corporations. Without even asking for intergovernmental approval, the Secretary-General established a new tent-like institution under his personal office for corporate executives to meet with each other and with senior UN officials. When in 2001 the UN General Assembly adopted its first Global Partnership resolution it made no mention of the Global Compact (UN 2002).[4] While the primary membership focus of the UN Global Compact was large TNCs, Annan felt that the formal governance structure should explicitly include representatives of international labor and civil society. The evolution of the UN Global Compact helped mark an important transition in the acceptance by TNCs of multistakeholder governance arrangements.

2002 was the next important year in the transformation of the relationship between multilateralism and the corporate world. In February, governments at the Financing for Development Conference largely reversed the omission of references to TNCs in the UN Charter by creating procedures to certify business organizations *in their own right* as conference participants (UN 2001). In June of that year, on the occasion of the 10th anniversary of the Rio Conference, governments created a new type of outcome from an intergovernmental conference. Corporations, civil society, governments, and others were welcomed to announce "Type II outcomes:" privately constructed public-private partnerships focused on the implementation of sustainable development goals.

The Global Recession and the development of the SDGs created even further opportunities for reciprocal UN-private sector engagement. The UN system announced multiple platforms for diverse active participation with TNCs in implementing intergovernmental goals. For their part, leading TNCs and their partner organizations declared that the UN system resolutions, as long as they were voluntary, were good guides for long-term market expansion. With each new resolution and each pro-UN corporate declaration, one can see the increasing recognition that TNCs should be seen as legitimate partners and actors in global governance.

A major counter-current to the warming engagement of the corporate sector toward the multilateral process involved tobacco. In the WHO Tobacco Convention, governments included an explicit statement that tobacco companies could not participate in negotiations of the convention and should not participate in national tobacco policy-setting (WHO 2003: Article 5.3).

Transformation of the relationship between NGOs/CSOs and the UN system

Over the same period, there has also been a transition in the relationship between non-state, non-commercial organizations and the UN system. These changes in the role that NGOs and CSOs play as "regular" participants in intergovernmental meetings have been accompanied by a corresponding change in the vocabulary.

In the UN Charter, all potential non-state actors can apply to be "Non-Governmental Organizations with Consultative Status to the Economic and Social Council" (ECOSOC) (UN 1945). Over the years ECOSOC has established an explicit set of procedures to allow governments to decide whether a given NGO could be granted the formal status. During the 1950s and 1960s, the Cold War and the North–South split polarized the approval of NGOs for this special status. The multi-year approval process meant that most of the organizations approved by ECOSOC were in fact international professional organizations and the process effectively excluded organizations that did not have a strong institutional base. In addition, the UN Charter only envisioned non-state actors working with just one part of the UN – solely the ECOSOC – not with the General Assembly, the Security Council, or any other part of the UN system. By the time of the major international conferences of the 1990s, however, UN system intergovernmental bodies had established their own procedures to decide which NGOs/CSOs could be accredited to each conference or intergovernmental body. All of these arrangements have non-state bodies serving in an advisory or expert consultant role to an intergovernmental process or that organization's secretariat.

As with the transformation of the relationship between the international corporate sector and the UN system, the 1992 Rio Conference marked a turning point in the organization of the relationship between civil society and the UN system. Maurice Strong saw that a broad range of non-governmental actors could prod governments to take a more creative approach to the issue of environment and development. He created on his own authority the nine-constituent Major Group category.[5] This Major Group structure facilitated two inter-related processes. First, it facilitated greater clarity for governments to hear common statements from CSOs on a given agenda item. Second, it provided an opportunity for the nine constituency categories to interact with each other on a peer-to-peer basis, something that the separate constituency groups had not often done. These Major Groups were referenced in the Rio outcome declaration and subsequently became active multi-constituent groups in other UN meetings, including the Commission on Sustainable Development and the High-Level Political Forum on Sustainable Development.

By the mid-1980s, however, it became clear that these organizations did not want to be known as what they were not i.e., "non-governmental

38 *A convergence of multiple trends*

organizations," but rather by a name that reflected the social forces they were part of. A variety of names from "Major Groups" to "social movements" were explored before the current "civil society organizations" captured their new relationship with the UN system.

Elsewhere in the UN, changes were also occurring in the relationship between intergovernmental bodies and civil society. For instance, the FAO Committee on Food Security (CFS) broke new ground by establishing a multi-constituency program to help the FAO deal with a major global crisis. Rather than convening another intergovernmental event, the CFS opened a wide door to learn from social movements – fisherfolk, women farmers, international health advocates, and other un- and under-heard agricultural constituencies – about how they felt the global food supply should function. These communities worked both together and separately to formulate new conceptual and organizational responses to global food security in ways that governments at the FAO recognized would bring significant benefit to themselves and the FAO (McKeon 2015).

Currently, one almost expects that intergovernmental bodies, conferences of the parties to international conventions, and the UN system secretariats will use this more open and engaging framework to engage with the non-commercial world. However, as previously noted, these *multi-constituency* arrangements have often been mislabelled as *multistakeholder* processes, creating a retrospective legitimacy for autonomous multistakeholder groups which are not at all interested in simply "advising" governments or "consulting" with ECOSOC.

Not all CSOs have welcomed this change. Some are disillusioned by the perceived political impotence of the intergovernmental system. Others re-prioritized their efforts to directly confront – or work with – TNCs or their national governments on global crises.

However, the net impact has been that CSOs, members of the Major Groups, professional associations, religious bodies, and members of the academy all came to see themselves as legitimate participants in global governance. Multi-constituency bodies provide a conducive vehicle for each member of the group to participate in global governance. Each constituency could in theory participate without arguing that other constituencies should be excluded. And each constituency could see themselves – and be seen by governments – as having a stake in solving global issues. The acceptance of other constituencies as possible legitimate actors in global governance involved a shift even in organizations that had a long antagonistic history.

Transformation of the relationship between CSOs and TNCs

The overall relationship between national and international NGOs and TNCs from the end of WWII to the 1980s can best be described as confrontational, if not antagonistic. Whether supporting anti-colonial battles against mining firms, organizing boycotts against firms cooperating with Apartheid, supporting labor unions against foreign investors, organizing against wars that were benefiting TNCs, or insisting that TNC factories should not pollute the environment – the relationship between TNCs and civil society was shaped by an on-going series of battles. In return, TNCs engaged in aggressive public campaigns to delegitimize NGOs.

The recent shift in the nature of the relationship between CSOs and TNCs has been dramatic. In the standard-setting world Dingwerth and Pattberg (2009: 708) noted:

> [New standard-setting groups involving CSOs and TNCs] also exemplify a strategic shift of transnational non-governmental organizations from lobbying rulemakers to making and implementing the rules themselves.

Similar transformations occurred with project-based multistakeholder projects where TNCs recruited local and international civil society organizations to participate in PPPs.

In some places, combatants in a struggle over natural resources chose to negotiate directly with the international mining industry rather than lobbying a national government to act or appealing to UNCTAD or UNIDO (the United Nations Industrial Development Organization) to take on an issue. Others, worried about the shortage of financial resources to address a particular global or regional issue, went directly to private sector foundations, individual corporate philanthropies, or private sector banks to get financial backing, rather than waiting for a government to find resources in bilateral aid budgets or to convince the World Bank to fund a project. Some other concerned leaders saw that working with major commercial actors directly could lead to environmental or health and safety standards being put in place better – or certainly faster –than convening a WHO or FAO intergovernmental expert group to make non-binding recommendations to the international community. Others considered that getting two to five TNCs and their 200–500 affiliates around the world acting in a better environmental or social fashion was wiser than advocating at the UN for new soft law.

Greenpeace began working with individual TNCs on climate change; Unilever approached the World Wildlife Fund (WWF) to work together on saving marine resources; international business organizations and the World Resources Institute (WRI) undertook joint work on a range of climate-related measurement projects; the Stakeholder Forum hosted gatherings of CSO leaders and TNCs; and WEF-sponsored conferences extended invitations to leaders of international and national CSOs. For both categories of organizations, the direct and public engagement between individual TNCs and TNC-sponsored bodies and civil society organizations was significant. Some CSOs created separate sections for working

40 *A convergence of multiple trends*

with TNCs and separate sections for working against the corporate sector. Similarly, some TNCs had units that worked with CSOs while other parts of the firm had little or nothing to do with CSOs. The shift caused a split within the TNC world and a split within the CSO world between those organizations which opted to work with the other communities and those which distrusted anyone who elected to work across the barriers.

Transformation of the corporate belief that the management of globalization may need a global quasi-state function

Since the sharp rise of TNCs following WWII, TNCs have been very clear that governments should not set any non-trade-related rules for the international market. After the start of the 2008/2009 recession, a number of TNCs and TNC-related elite bodies have altered their view and recognized that some form of quasi-state function is needed for globalization. Their changed perspective is based in part on one of the arguments for state intervention in domestic markets and for anti-competition laws. At times, the state needs to save-capitalism-from-itself. The "natural" monopolization of markets, it is said, would result in the sharp loss of competition, a decrease in real wages, and a reduction in productivity. Following this line of thought, the function of the state in the economy is in part to intervene to ensure a reasonable level of domestic competition in order for capitalism to continue to function, and on the other hand to arbitrate between public demands for social and humanitarian needs and firm-centered practices. Individual firms, particularly those holding a dominant role in a given sector, would complain bitterly and undertake all sorts of actions to dissuade states from supporting enhanced regulation. To the extent that states have the capacity to control their domestic economy, the argument is that this state power was able to keep national capitalism in good shape.

The international market, however, is fundamentally different from any single domestic market. There is no analogous body to the nation-state at the international level; consequently, the international market has no institution capable of preventing the over-monopolization of a market and no institution with the capacity to balance the drivers of the commercial market with the human and ecological needs of a global population. Globally dominant TNCs through the 1970s, 1980s, and 1990s introduced the oxymoronic concept of "self-regulation" to fend off ideological and practical demands for some level of effective global market intervention.

By the early 2000s, Utting noted the beginning of the realization by the corporate world that some quasi-state global institution was necessary for the sake of globalization:

> [Some business leaders] ... recognized the limits of corporate self-regulation and various forms of voluntary initiatives: too many

different standards were being designed and voluntary initiatives that relied on corporate self-regulation were losing credibility, as well as their ability to realize basic objectives related to reputation and risk management.

(Utting 2002)

In 2010, WEF's GRI report explicitly recognized the need for a quasi-global state function to monitor globalization, much in the same way that national economies have been regulated. The GRI argued that without joint governance ventures with with civil society and governments to re-assert effectiveness and legitimacy for globalization, systemic tensions would continue to challenge the foundations of the global market and international relations.

The GRI study also offered a number of examples of how the de facto informal economic global governance processes could be better managed by TNCs united with governments under the auspices of the UN system. The thinking proffered that if globalization leaders were more involved in the policy development and program implementation of the UN, then organizations and peoples throughout the world may well consider these combined efforts to be more legitimate. The benefits of conjoining the informal market-based governance system with the official state-centered system included that TNCs would no longer be outside the recognized governance gate but would enter the system as equal or greater partners to governments in a transformed UN system (Gleckman 2013).

Calls for some new quasi-state global governance system have also emanated from a range of newer economic sectors. On the technology side, certain technological industries feel they need more than ISO product standardization to be fully effective on a global scale (e.g., IT, geoengineering). On the financial side, the interconnectedness of significant financial institutions prompted central bankers to call for a new global identification system and a new globally agreed definition of financial assets and risks. On the foreign direct investment side, the proliferation of bilateral investment treaties containing provisions that foreign investors can sue states directly for potential losses from new state regulations or national laws is in effect the establishment of an international, quasi-court system over nation-states. On the private investment side, some leading investors recognized that there was a lack of proper incentives to channel capital into globally important long-term institutional investments (Aviva 2017). Jack Ma, the founder of Chinese e-commerce giant Alibaba, has proposed a new business-led initiative for framing global e-commerce rules (Ma 2017). These developments reflect a growing awareness that some form of internationally coordinated interventions are necessary to hold international capital, insurance, and technology markets together in the long run.

Parminder Jeet Singh summarized this transformation from a critical perspective:

And to the extent that certain policy/lawmaking simply cannot be done without involving some social actors other than just the mega businesses, there is a new kind of business-led process of policy/lawmaking called multi-stakeholderism. It co-opts select government and civil society actors who can bless the business-dictated frameworks, with a few concessions thrown here and there to the co-opted parties....

(Singh 2016)

Recognition of multistakeholderism as a governance form

The recognition of multistakeholderism as a new form of governance entailed the introduction of "stakeholder" as a governance actor, the generalization by elite bodies of their practice of multistakeholderism, the declaration that early multistakeholder experiments were successful, and the welcome of multistakeholderism by the existing governance system, multilateralism.

The evolution of "stakeholder" as a concept of governance

The concept of "stakeholder," born in the world of gambling, has been introduced into the day-to-day language of government and business policy-making. Stakeholder terminology has come to mean that advocates of a constituency (for instance, labor groups, the elderly, women), advocates for a global concern (such as climate change, the protection of forests, child health), and advocates for an institution (including governments, businesses, or religious institutions) have standing in global governance. Some of these constituencies are already represented as citizens by their government.

The word "stakeholder" itself has an interesting and relevant history. Wikipedia (2017) reports that:

> The role of stakeholder is a concept in law. A stakeholder was originally a person who temporarily holds money or other property while its owner is being determined. This is, for example, the situation when two persons bet on the outcome of a future event and ask a third, disinterested, neutral person to hold the money (or "stake[s]") that they have wagered (or "staked"). After the event occurs, the stakeholder distributes the stakes to one or both of the original (or other) parties according to the outcome of the event and according to the previously decided conditions.

It is not clear when the terminology of stakeholder first moved from the world of gambling to the world of economics and politics. One view considers that it entered political and social discourse at about the same time as corporate social responsibility (CSR). CSR has its roots in labor struggles in the UK, when trade unions argued that companies had a responsibility not just to their shareholders, but also social responsibilities to the workers.

In the economic business sphere, the term helped corporate executives and corporate board members see that there were social forces whose actions and views could have a significant impact on their core markets and financial profitability. One version of this approach is contained in the work of Klaus Schwab, the founder and director of the World Economic Forum. This is particularly relevant since WEF – through its Global Redesign Initiative – has become a major advocate for multistakeholder governance.

For Schwab, the concept of the stakeholder is centered on the corporation and institutions that affect corporate actions. Schwab outlined this idea in 1971, and restated it in 2009 in his book, *The First Forty Years* (Schwab 2009), writing that the "management of the modern enterprise must serve all stakeholders (die Interessenten) acting as their trustee charged with achieving the long-term sustained growth and prosperity of the company." *The First Forty Years* emphasized this corporate-centered view with a graphic from Schwab's 1971 book. The graphic shows "the company" in the center with ovals from top to bottom that read "shareholders" (owners), "creditors," "customers," "national economy," "government and society," "suppliers," and "collaborators." The four crucial elements of what WEF and other corporate management teams mean by stakeholders are embedded here: first, that multistakeholder structures do not mean equal roles for all stakeholders; second, that the institution of the corporation is at the center of the process; third, that engaging stakeholders is seen as strengthening the corporation; and fourth, that the list of important multistakeholders contains principally those with commercial ties to the company, including customers, creditors, suppliers, collaborators, owners, and national economies. All the rest of the potential stakeholders are grouped together as "government and society."

The transition between the gambling version of the definition of a stakeholder to the corporate-centered version seems to have evolved in an interesting way. Those wanting corporate executives and board members to recognize that they have broader obligations than just to their investors had the challenge to shift the conversation in a non-threatening fashion. One aspect of this battle to get the corporate world to recognize the impact of the firm on other constituencies seems quite linguistic. Proponents of engaging corporate-related constituencies only needed to change two letters, shifting smoothly from "shareholder" to "stakeholder."

Subsequently the term moved into the domestic political world with government agencies seeking to engage "stakeholders" in their own work. The stakeholders identified were those who had a tie to an organization, this time a particular government department. As with the corporate use of the stakeholder concept, the governmental use also involved bringing in social constituencies to learn their views and activities, particularly those whose perspectives were not captured sufficiently by elections, traditional lobbying activities, or other outreach activities. This process was intended to result in a more effective – or less controversial role – for the government agency.

When the multistakeholder ISO, which sets technical and process standards for the majority of products in international trade, created a standard for corporate social responsibility (ISO 26000), it defined "stakeholder" as an "individual or group that has an interest in any decision or activity of an organization" (ISO 26000, 2014: 2.1.12). ISEAL, the trade support group for environmental and social standard-setting multistakeholder groups, adopted the ISO definition in its code of good practice (ISEAL 2014: 7). As with the corporate and government approach, "stakeholder" for the ISO and ISEAL is tied to a specific "organization." It also introduces a new term – "interest" – which, while not further defined, opens the term "stakeholder" up to an exceptionally wide collection of "individuals" and "groups."

The transition of the term stakeholder from one centered on an organization to "international multistakeholder governance" involved another series of significant moves.

In multistakeholder governance, there is no longer a central institution, meaning no TNC or government agency which seeks to engage stakeholders to perform the central institution's function better. Multistakeholder governance now refers to a self-standing body, disconnected from any other institution. The prior advisor-consultant stakeholders are now running an institution for themselves. In the shift to international multistakeholderism, the members of the multistakeholder group are no longer providing input to a corporation, government agency, or UN body, but instead are leaders who will themselves use the information in their role within a multistakeholder governance process.

In current multistakeholder parlance, the terminology now differentiates between multistakeholder categories (e.g., workers, TNCs, governments) and multistakeholder organizations or participants (e.g., the International Confederation of Free Trade Unions, Microsoft, and Argentina). The main purpose of this differentiation is to distinguish the category of governance actor engaged with a multistakeholder group from the name of the specific organization or participant designated to be the spokesperson for that stakeholder category. This differentiation is central to the practice of multistakeholderism by international elite business-related bodies – the majority of the people they expect to be in the room represent "business" interests and the minority represent different stakeholder categories.

The birth of elite corporate bodies with a multistakeholder perspective

Elite international bodies have a long-standing history. From the old-line Bilderberg Group, to the politically focused Trilateral Commission, to socially restricted private clubs, the growth of international capitalism has created special spaces for face-to-face elite peer communities. What has happened more recently is that some of these special spaces have welcomed in a diversity of new faces while keeping stable their central elite membership.

Whether it is the WEF at Davos inviting in high-level elected officials, civil society leaders and celebrities, the Internet Corporation for Assigned Names and Numbers (ICANN) in the governance of technology welcoming in technologically savvy younger scientists and critics, or the Bill and Melinda Gates Foundation inviting in government leaders from recipient countries and health advocates to set health policies for the Global Vaccine Alliance (GAVI), elite international bodies have selectively opened the door to multiple new constituencies while keeping overall control of the organization. While selected by elite bodies, these new constituencies and their designated representatives generate a public enthusiasm for better cross-cultural, cross-social, and cross-technological engagement.

The WEF engagement with multistakeholder-style governance grew out of over four decades of experience with the annual WEF gatherings in Davos Klosters and two decades of regional meetings in four continents. These WEF events nurtured an informal environment between the invited leaders from governments, international business, professional bodies, the scientific community, international civil society, and popular culture. As the three WEF leaders observed in their introduction to the GRI: "The time has come for a new stakeholder paradigm of international governance analogous to that embodied in the stakeholder theory of corporate governance on which the World Economic Forum itself was founded" (WEF 2010: 9).

In the WEF's view, multinationals, governments, and civil society have evolved as relatively independent governance spaces on the international level. The economic governance space is dominated by corporations, while governments and the wider public focus their attention on the UN system. The civil society governance space, as seen by WEF, is one that is successful in defining new issues and acting to transmit messages and ideas to and from important communities. One of the key premises of the GRI is that the separation of key political actors on the global scene has changed and that through a "new geography of governance" they can jointly manage a globalized world better – and ought to do so.

The GRI report argues that systemic tensions will continue to challenge the foundations of the global market and international relations without such joint ventures to reassert effectiveness and legitimacy for globalization. A new global governance partnership structure clearly entails some quite radical changes for the United Nations and its specialized agencies. This integration of global executives with UN diplomats and international civil servants is seen as a way to rejuvenate the acceptance of globalization. The early multistakeholder groups were seen as confirming these views.

First movers deemed successful

Major OECD governments, the UN system and the international media created great fanfare around the first successful multistakeholder groups.

Early groups in the peace and security field included the Kimberly Process Certification Scheme; in the environmental field the Type II outcomes from the 2002 Johannesburg Earth Summit; in the development of ethical market standards the Forest Stewardship Council; in the corporate disclosure field the Global Reporting Initiative; in the health field UNAIDS; in the large-scale infrastructure field the Commission on Dams; and in the technology management field ICANN. Recognition of these successes came from many different directions. The General Assembly adopted a series of resolutions supporting the Kimberly Process as the way to address a regional armed conflict even though the subject matter is usually the exclusive preserve of the Security Council. The UN Department of Economic and Social Affairs lauded the Type II outcomes as major milestones in international affairs while they understated the official outcomes which include only a few significant advances over the original 1992 Rio Conference on Environment and Development. Even the US Congress welcomed the success of ICANN when it "Express[ed] the sense of Congress regarding actions to preserve and advance the multistakeholder governance model under which the Internet has thrived" (US Congress 2012). Three years later a senior official in the US Department of State's Bureau of Economic and Business Affairs conveyed a more direct endorsement. She argued that "Every meeting that is enriched by multistakeholder participation serves as an example and a precedent that opens doors for multistakeholder participation in future meetings and fora" (Zoller 2015).

The enthusiasm for multistakeholder implementation is sufficiently strong that a public evaluation of the effectiveness of one of the first movers in UN-sponsored multistakeholder initiatives was blocked by the Commission on Sustainable Development (CSD). The CSD set such significant obstacles to an official review of Type II outcomes that the review never happened. Subsequently, a series of civil society and academic studies confirmed that almost all of the Type II goals were not delivered. In fact, the UN system has never published a rigorous evaluation of a multistakeholder policy project or a public-private partnership involving a UN body.

The enthusiasm for multistakeholder-led initiatives also constrained the acknowledgement that another first mover, the Kimberley Process, simply collapsed. When its multistakeholder governing body would not decertify Zimbabwe, the last of the three founding civil society organizations involved dropped out, leaving only the diamond industry and selected African countries involved in the process (Global Witness 2011). At the time of writing, the level of daily violence related to diamonds and other African natural resources remains a threat to people living in the region.

However, the public image of "successful" multistakeholder groups remains crucial to building acceptance of this new form of governance, particularly inside the international community and the UN system.

Welcoming by the intergovernmental system of multi-constituency consultations and non-state global leadership

The multilateral system discovered the clear benefits that arise from multi-constituency open consultations. When civil society leaders, corporate executives, and other leading figures developed new ideas and advocated effectively for them, governments and the UN Secretariat recognized that the resulting resolutions, conventions, and programs of work are clearly stronger.

The multilateral system has also discovered that multistakeholderism can be a complement to, or a surrogate for, their constrained opportunities for global action. In some ways, governmental failures on the part of the multilateral system have been a self-inflicted injury. Without a sizeable commitment of financial resources and a strong political commitment to multilateralism, government delegates have very limited options for actually implementing a solution to a complicated global issue.

In these circumstances, governments and international governing bodies have welcomed both multi-constituency engagement and multistakeholder implementation. In his 2000 Millennium Report, the UN Secretary-General Kofi Annan made a clear call for multi-constituency engagement under the umbrella of multilateralism:

> ... the international public domain – including the United Nations – must accept the participation of the many actors whose contributions are essential to managing the path of globalisation. Depending on the issues at hand, this may include civil society organisations, the private sector, parliamentarians, local authorities, scientific associations, educational institutions, and many others.
>
> (Annan 2000: 6, as cited in West 2006: 155–56)

To carry out this thinking, the Secretary-General established a commission under former Brazilian President Fernando Henrique Cardoso to institutionalize the UN's connection with the various non-state sectors (UN 2004). The Cardoso Commission's institutional arrangements were ultimately not accepted, as they provoked a variety of intra-secretariat disputes and external governmental concerns. The report, however, elevated the importance of non-state actors as policy-makers and program implementers for UN institutions.

48 *A convergence of multiple trends*

Even the World Trade Organization (WTO), when its members faced a major negotiation problem, welcomed using a multistakeholder group to help find a legal solution. WTO members wished to prevent other governments from prioritizing domestic products through the use of national regulatory systems. In response, government members circumvented the multilateral process and agreed to follow recommendations made by the multistakeholder ISO (Krut and Gleckman 1998). In this manner, the multilateral trade regime granted full legitimacy and legal authority to the rulings of a multistakeholder organization.

The process of the multilateral system blessing the decisions of autonomous multistakeholder groups is complemented by the practice of the UN system outsourcing implementation of intergovernmental decisions to multiple external actors. Multi-constituency engagement indicated that governments and international organizations could channel public concerns toward the multilateral system without expending political capital, financial resources, or taking politically tough decisions. The outsourcing of implementation to multistakeholders culminated in a discrete SDG target on multistakeholder partnerships. SDG 17, target 1 aims to:

- Enhance the global partnership for sustainable development, complemented by multistakeholder partnerships that mobilize and share knowledge, expertise, technology and financial resources, to support the achievement of the sustainable development goals in all countries, in particular developing countries
- Encourage and promote effective public, public-private and civil society partnerships, building on the experience and resourcing strategies of partnerships (UN 2015)

Intergovernmental bodies can identify a problem and then wait – or call – for multistakeholder bodies to establish a response, a new organization or a new funding mechanism. If things are going well with a multistakeholder initiative, international governing bodies can extend their blessing to these undertakings.

Macro-forces creating a new political platform for global governance

Each of these twelve trends in its own unique way played a crucial role in creating the space for a new global platform for governance. In combination they made the appearance of multistakeholder governance seem like the reasonable next step after multilateralism.

The disillusion with multilateralism – whether well founded or not – set the psychological stage for the search for a post-nation-state-based global governance system. In the various governance reports in the past decade, one can see how the case for multistakeholder governance is often made by first citing a range of "failures" of multilateralism and then moving without evidence to the assertion that the new system can actually fill these claimed governance and organizational gaps.

The transformation in relationships – whether between NGOs/CSOs and the UN, between the private sector and the UN, or between international civil society and the commercial sector – created the political terrain for a qualitatively different arrangement in governance. At the end of WWII, the private sector did not appear on the official geopolitical terrain. By the 2000s, however, TNCs and the UN system had found multiple rationales for joint recognition. When the UN Charter was adopted, civil society was simply that which was not a nation-state. By the mid-1990s, civil society engagement with the UN system was almost a requisite requirement for any serious intergovernmental meeting.

To denote the new platform, a new vocabulary appeared. This provided two complementary elements to the new system of global governance. By labelling public hearings and outreach as "multistakeholder," the term provided a "history" to the concept and a claim to legitimacy. At the same time, a phrase was introduced that, while comfortable to many actors in the world of global governance, had little clear meaning.

Success, and the perception of success, played its own role in making it feel that multistakeholder governance was a natural next step in global governance. UN delegates, constrained by domestic political ideologies and financial budgetary limitations, could continue to articulate standards knowing that success could only come from other actors delivering on their goals. Elite international organizations, recognizing that talking only to themselves had diminishing returns, discovered that they could have greater success if they brought into their elite homes a selected number of non-elite actors. And multistakeholderism managed to convey success for handling specific global crises; even when a number of the claimed multistakeholder successes were functional failures, the momentum continued to grow.

The conjuncture of these political developments has generated a global experimental platform for multistakeholderism, whose internal beliefs and structural characteristics are explored further in Chapter 3.

Notes

1 The only recent exception is UNWomen. The other two new members of the UN system, The International Renewable Energy Agency (IRENA) and the International Organization for Migration (IOM), were pre-existing organizations.
2 With the exception that the major governments created the G20 in order to better coordinate their own positions.
3 Now called the World Business Council for Sustainable Development.
4 It was six more years before the General Assembly made its first formal statement containing a recognition of the Global Compact (UN 2008).
5 Women, Children and Youth, Indigenous Peoples, Non-Governmental Organizations, Local Authorities, Workers and Trade Unions, Business and Industry, Scientific and Technological Community, and Farmers.

References

Aviva. 2017. A Roadmap for Sustainable Capital Markets: How can the UN Sustainable Development Goals harness the global capital markets? – An Aviva White Paper, London, October 27, 2017.

Dingwerth, Klaus and Philipp Pattberg. 2009. "World Politics and Organizational Fields: The Case of Transnational Sustainability Governance." *European Journal of International Relations* 15, no. 4: 707–44.

ECOSOC 1974. Economic and Social Commission Resolution: The Impact of Transnational Corporations on the Development Process and on International Relations 1913 (LVII).

FAO. 2017. "Freedom From Hunger Project: The Industry Cooperative Program." Last modified September 6, 2017. Available from https://freedomfromhunger-project.weebly.com/the-industry-cooperative-programme.html.

Gleckman, Harris. 2012. "Readers' Guide: Global Redesign Initiative." Boston: Center for Governance and Sustainability at the University of Massachusetts Boston. Available from www.umb.edu/gri.

Gleckman, Harris. 2013. "WEF Proposes a Public-Private United 'Nations.'" *Policy Innovations*, June 18, 2013. Available from www.carnegiecouncil.org/publications/archive/policy_innovations/commentary/000263.GlobalWitness. 2011. "Global Witness Leaves Kimberly Process, Calls for Diamond Trade to be Held Accountable." London: Global Witness.

Hamdani, Khalil and Lorraine Ruffing. 2015. *United Nations Centre on Transnational Corporations: Corporate Conduct and the Public Interest* (Global Institutions). London: Routledge.

International Federation for Human Rights. 2016. "EU/Migration: the answer is neither militarization nor outsourcing." Available from www.fidh.org/en/issues/migrants-rights/eu-migration-the-answer-is-neither-militarization-nor-outsourcing.

ISEAL. 2014. Setting Social and Environmental Standards: ISEAL Code of Good Practice, Version 6.0. London.

ISO (International Organization for Standardization). 2014. Guidance on social responsibility: ISO 26000. ISO/TMB/WG SR N 172. Geneva.

ISS. 2010. *Global Governance 2025: At a Critical Juncture*. Paris: Institute for Security Studies European Union with National Intelligence Council.

Krut, Riva and Harris Gleckman. 1998. *ISO 14001: A Missed Opportunity for Sustainable Global Industrial Development*. London: Earthscan.

Ma, Jack. 2017, "Too early to regulate e-commerce", *The Hindu*, December 12, 2017.

McKeon, Nora. 2015. *Food Security Governance: Empowering Communities, Regulating Corporations*. London: Routledge.

OECD. 2008. "OECD Guidelines for Multinational Enterprises." Paris: Organization for Economic Cooperation and Development.

Singh, Parminder Jeet. 2016. "A borderless economy that will be controlled." *The Hindu*, May 11, 2016.

Schwab, Klaus. 2009. "World Economic Forum. A Partner in Shaping History: The First 40 Years." Davos: The World Economic Forum.

TNI. 2017. "Understanding and Confronting Authoritarianism – Meeting Report." Amsterdam: Transnational Institute Amsterdam.

UN. 1945. *Charter of the United Nations*, UN DC 1 UNTS XV (October 24, 1945).
UN. 2001. Preparations for the substantive preparatory process and the International Conference on Financing for Development, GA Agenda Item 101, UN GA 55th session, UN Doc A/RES/55/245 (distributed April 23, 2001).
UN. 2002. *Towards Global Partnerships*, GA Agenda Item 39, UN GA 56th session, UN Doc A/56/76 (distributed January 24, 2002).
UN. 2004. *Strengthening of the United Nations System: Note by the Secretary-General*, GA Agenda Item 59, UN GA 58th session, UN Doc A/58/817 (distributed June 11, 2004).
UN. 2008 Towards global partnerships GA Res 62/211, UN GA 62nd session, UN Doc A/RES/62/211 (March 11, 2008; adopted December 19, 2007).
UN. 2015. *Transforming our World: the 2030 Agenda for Sustainable Development*, GA Res 70/1, UN GA, 70th session, UN Doc A/RES/70/1 (October 21, 2015; adopted September 25, 2015).
UNFCCC. 2017. "The Paris Agreement." Last modified June 20, 2017. Available from http://unfccc.int/paris_agreement/items/9485.php.
UNFCCC. n.d. "KP Introduction." Accessed February 9, 2018. Available from http://unfccc.int/kyoto_protocol/items/2830.php.
US Congress. 2012. H.Con.Res.127 Expressing the sense of Congress regarding actions to preserve and advance the multistakeholder governance model under which the Internet has thrived. 112th Congress. Washington DC: May 30, 2012.
Utting, Peter. 2002. "Regulating Business Via Multistakeholder Initiatives: A Preliminary Assessment." Geneva: UN Non-Governmental Liaison Service (NGLS) and UNRISD.
WEF. 2010. "Global Redesign: Strengthening International Cooperation in a More Interdependent World." Geneva: World Economic Forum.
West, John. 2006. "Multistakeholder Diplomacy at the OECD." In Kurbalija, J. and Katrandjiev, V. (eds) *Multistakeholder Diplomacy: Challenges and Opportunities*. Malta: DiploFoundation, 149–63.
WHO. 2003. "Who Framework Convention on Tobacco Control." Geneva: World Health Organization.
Wikipedia. 2017. "Stakeholder (law)" Accessed November 10, 2017. Available from https://en.wikipedia.org/wiki/Stakeholder.
Zoller, Julie. 2015. "Advancing the Multistakeholder Approach in the Multilateral Context." Speech given at The Marvin Center at George Washington University, July 16, 2015, Washington DC: US Government Position.

3 Global actors from multilateralism to multistakeholderism

Governance actors from yesterday to tomorrow

For over 400 years the centrality of the nation-state was the guiding principle of international relations. All other institutional forces formally recognized that governments were the exclusive official actor in global governance. In the field of international relations, academics and government foreign service officers studied the interface between nation-states and their militaries, their economic power, their political power, and their cultural power as the best way to understanding global governance. Following the end of WWII, governments established the key elements of contemporary multilateralism and intergovernmental organizations while TNCs exerted power which was increasingly autonomous from the nation-state in the global market. Military power remained largely in government hands, even when it was used to assert control over commercially valuable natural resources. In recent decades, a series of new actors are asserting that they should join the official process of global governance.

In a national context, the status of TNCs and CSOs is derivative and dependent on the nation-state which registers them and grants them their legal status. In the context of multilateralism, both institutions can act variously as advisors, lobbyists, consultants, partners with or challengers to governments. In multistakeholderism, actors now assert that in certain circumstances they should have a status similar to – or even greater than – that of nation-states in global governance. In other cases, non-state actors assert that they have not taken on governmental authority but nonetheless act as if they were state authorities.

In marked change from the multilateral world, in the multistakeholder world the basic governing unit is a "stakeholder," not the nation-state. Phrased in a different way, multistakeholderism is seeking to displace the nation-state and by implication the UN system as the central actors in international relations. "Stakeholders" are asserting their status as new global governors. Many of those involved in multistakeholder groups (MSGs) may not necessarily see themselves – or want to see themselves – as "global governors," but it is probably the appropriate term for those making decisions that seek to impact the governance of globalization or the governance of the planet's ecology.

The first section of this chapter describes the major existing nation-state institutions in multilateralism. The second section examines the new roles that nation-states and other governance actors now have under a multistakeholder form of governance.

The advent of multistakeholderism as a potential next form of global governance invites the study of a number of unresolved – and maybe unresolvable – democratic challenges. As reviewed in this chapter, these democratic challenges include:

a   the foundational concept of "stakeholders" – this new governance category elevates selected participants to new roles without a clear democratic selection process or rationale;
b   boundaries around each stakeholder category – the boundaries of each potential stakeholder group are ambiguous and ill defined. A given stakeholder can claim correctly to be in multiple categories;
c   the role of the convener – There is no analogous institution in national democracies for these new gatekeepers, who have a central role in selecting global governors and in drafting the terms of reference for individual MSGs;
d   the selection of global governance participants – this process has clear opportunities for conflicts of interest and high barriers to participation by politically marginal but affected communities;
e   the role of TNCs and CSOs – these governing actors, central to multistakeholderism, have no equivalent status in any national democratic parliament;
f   the asymmetries of power between stakeholder categories – each category of potential stakeholders will bring into an MSG a different form of power. Whether these power differences can be partially equalized inside an MSG determines the extent to which a given MSG has the essential capacity for internally sensitive democratic decision-making; and
g   the potential change in holders of international obligations, responsibilities, and liabilities – as global decision-making shifts to some combination of different international actors, the potential reallocation of obligations, responsibilities and liabilities could significantly shift democratic accountability.

The institutional foundation for global governance

In the 400 years since the Treaty of Westphalia, nation-states have developed a series of rules to engage with other nation-states that cemented the centrality of the nation-state in international relations. In democratic theory, citizens are represented in international affairs by their national governments. Of course, these nation-states could wage war between themselves. When not engaged in inter-state warfare, the nation-state could work directly with one other country (bilateral relations); with a group of countries in the same geographic region (regional relations); with groups of countries with similar geographic or political characteristics (e.g., the association of landlocked developing countries); with a group of nation-states on a specific topic (e.g., global monetary management); with a group of nation-states to compete or dominate other nation-states (e.g., the North Atlantic Treaty Organization, NATO); and with all nation-states under one institutional umbrella (e.g., multilateralism).

Even with the myriad of formal mechanisms intended to build cooperation between nation-states, military power, war, and aggressive economic competition did not disappear. In practice, colonialism, capitalism, authoritarianism, and imperialism have taken precedence over cooperative institutional forms of nation-state relations. In so doing, this has created an on-going structural crisis between the ideological foundations for democracy and the reality where certain nation-states have exerted power over other nation-states and peoples.

Roughly over the same period, the practice of statecraft produced a body of international law regarding nation-state obligations, liabilities and responsibilities.[1] What is now called "hard law" consists of legally binding treaties and conventions and other obligatory frameworks. Each binding treaty or convention has gone through a process of inter-state negotiation followed by formal adoption by each nation-state's domestic political procedures. In most cases, conventions also create separate governing bodies and secretariats to oversee the terms of the agreement. Some of the institutional practices that developed over the centuries for appropriate nation-state behavior have been codified in a series of Vienna Conventions.[2] Even the rules of war between nation-states were codified in a series of Geneva Conventions.[3]

Legally binding agreements, however, cover only a limited number of scenarios involving relations between nation-states, or the relations between nation-states and citizens of other nation-states. Over time, the international legal community developed a less binding set of rules termed "soft law" (Abbot and Snidal 2009). Soft law is the accepted summary of what is the appropriate behavior on any given matter as reflected in the daily practices of a significant number of nation-states. Soft law also includes formal articulations of policy positions by intergovernmental bodies. Each intergovernmental body has its own practice in approving policy statements. These practices range from unanimous consensus agreements in economic-related bodies, to majority agreements in other non-economic bodies, to weighted voting outcomes in peace and security matters.

Within the UN system, there are also specific formal rule books and informal rules governing the engagement of nation-states and their delegates in intergovernmental bodies. The UN system rule books consider a range of actions, from the appropriate way to accredit delegates to intergovernmental meetings to protecting the political space of small countries in an intergovernmental meeting. These rules translate the formal equality of nation-states in multilateralism, a core Westphalian principle, into daily practice. The formal equality of nation-states is a clear statement of democratic interest in global governance.[4]

Intergovernmental structures

Starting in early 1943, well before the outcome of WWII was clear, the US and the UK convened a series of meetings to define post-war multilateral cooperation on monetary and financial matters, institutionalized later as the Bretton Woods Institutions (BWIs); cooperation on political and military matters, which became the UN; and the next phase of cooperation in trade, which resulted in the creation of the Generalized Agreement on Tariffs and Trade (GATT).[5] Concurrently, the military and ideological landscape created a range of military alliances (e.g., NATO and the Warsaw Pact) and prominent economic think-tanks (e.g., the OECD). Some significant alternative plans, such as the proposal for an International Trade Organization (Interim Commission for the International Trade Organization 1948) and the New International Economic Order (UN 1974) did not succeed in re-orienting the basic structure of the post-WWII institutions.

Additionally, some thirty other intergovernmental organizations were created after 1945 to address disparate tasks. The fragmentation between matters concerning finance, global social and ecological well-being, and peace and security was multiplied by the establishment of each new international organization. National health agencies work principally with the World Health Organization (WHO), national environmental ministries work closely with the United Nations Environment Programme (UNEP), and national trade offices focus their attention principally on the World Trade Organization (WTO). As a result, each department of government now has its "own" international organization.

Simultaneously, each international organization claims exclusive leadership over a different aspect of the global community, and, of course, competes for leadership on topics that overlap with the areas of work of other organizations. For example, the governance of food, the terrain of the Food and Agriculture Organization (FAO), also affects topics of global health, which is under the purview of the WHO. Similarly, international trade is the shared responsibility of the GATT/WTO and the UN Conference on Trade and Development (UNCTAD), and rural development is the joint responsibility of the World Bank and the United Nations Development Program (UNDP). The net effect has been that each major new global issue requires more ad hoc international coordination requirements.

Multistakeholder bodies are being established in part to bridge gaps in this system of international governance.

By the 1980s, the disconnect between the autonomy of each part of the UN, the IMF, the World Bank, and the specialized agencies was clearly unmanageable, even for the biggest proponents of individualized organizations. The UN Secretary-General could only voluntarily convene the heads of the staff of the UN system to discuss items of mutual interest. The Administrative Committee for Coordination and later the Chief Executives Board addressed areas of mutual concern to the heads of their organizations. Out of this process, the "UN system" and, for representation of the UN system in developing countries, "OneUN," was born. What was not established, however, was a parallel institution to coordinate at the intergovernmental level policy-setting and program design for all the bodies of the UN system.

The primary responsibility for coordinating intra-ministerial views and managing inter-country relations within a government generally falls to a ministry of foreign affairs or a department of state. When the topic for an international meeting or conference requires specialized knowledge, the ministry of foreign affairs can complement its team with staff from other ministries, and with additional professional advice from citizens, academics, or with advisors from the business community. In this fashion, the nation-state, in principle if not in practice, coordinates all its external affairs through one key ministry/department.[6] Over the past two decades, however, provinces and cities have been given opportunities to participate directly in intergovernmental meetings. In the sustainable development context, these local government bodies have been given a separate Major Group category; at the WTO sub-national bodies are directly addressed in official WTO agreements; and in the climate negotiations representatives of cities and towns have been given formal speaking opportunities. Some commentators have argued that provincial/state governments, counties, and municipalities should be able to sign and formally ratify intergovernmental agreements (Commission on Global Security, Justice, & Governance 2015: 50).

Multilateralism and all other forms of inter-state engagement are based on the centrality of nation-states as the international actor. The connection between citizens and their government is not actually relevant to the right of the nation-state to participate in international relations. Any government of a nation-state, even if it is not an elected one, is welcome to take part in the international system provided other governments formally approve them. It is certainly the case that governments, on behalf of their own nation-state, exclusively create hard law conventions and treaties, adopt soft law resolutions, create international organizations, and are seen by other governments as legitimate representatives of their nation-state and their citizens in international affairs. This hierarchical Westphalian system, however, is under challenge by multistakeholderism, which asserts that other actors should formally or informally undertake some of these roles in international relations.

Special governance arrangements under multilateralism

There are, however, international governance organizations where the nation-state is not now central. The importance of these outlier institutions is that they are examples of existing multilateral structures where governments are not the exclusive leaders. As such, these institutions serve to legitimate an important element of multistakeholderism, where the nation-state is in a secondary or non-exclusive leadership position in international decision-making.

The most well-known governance system outlier is the International Labour Organization (ILO). The ILO has established separate structures for governments, employers, and labor. The tri-partite ILO was created in a different era; it came into existence following the initial phase of the Russian revolution. There were major concerns in the rest of Europe and in North America that worker-based movements would overthrow governments and the capitalist economic system. Thus, the idea for a tri-partite governing structure for the ILO was to engage workers, employers, and governments in one organization so as to constrain the expansion of socialist labor organizations and to have a more stable labor market in the West. The ILO's governing body has twenty-eight government representatives, fourteen employer representatives, and fourteen worker representatives. Formally, the membership of the ILO consists of national governments, but each national delegation is obligated to have four members, two from the government and "two others ... representing the employers and the workpeople."[7] The employer and workpeople representatives from the separate national delegations select their representatives for the ILO governing body. This three-way political balancing system is implemented nowhere else in the UN system.

The second category of institutional outliers are large international standard-setting organizations. For instance, the International Organization for Standardization (ISO) sets technical standards for products and processes.[8] Legally, the ISO is a non-governmental organization made up of members from national standards bodies (Murphy and Yates 2009). Most national standards bodies are government agencies (like in Germany and in China); in other countries the national standards bodies are corporate sponsored institutions (like in the UK and in Japan). The core work of the ISO is done through Technical Committees, of which there are currently over 240 (ISO 2016). The national standard-setting bodies can appoint government staff, corporate volunteers, scientific experts, and public representatives to represent them on the Technical Committees. Given the political, commercial, and technological realities of standard-setting, the majority of these designated representatives are executives of firms and trade associations. As noted earlier, the standards set by the ISO are referenced by governments and the WTO.[9]

The third category of institutional outliers are science-based international governance organizations. One important contemporary example is the International Union for Conservation of Nature (IUCN).[10] The IUCN has three categories of members – governments and economic integration organizations, international NGOs, and national NGOs – and a weighted voting system between these constituencies. The IUCN amongst other activities prepares the "Red List of Threatened Species," which is the world's most comprehensive assessment of species that are at varying degrees of risk of extinction. IUCN's Red List and other similar lists are used by UNEP and the UN Convention on Biological Diversity as key reference documents.

Intergovernmental bodies and their secretariats

Legally, the secretariats in the UN system derive their legitimacy and authority from the intergovernmental body that directs their work. For instance, the World Health Assembly determines what the WHO Secretariat is authorized to do; the Commission on Crime Prevention and Criminal Justice provides the intergovernmental leadership to the UN Office on Drugs and Crime; and the General Assembly approves resolutions that often end with assignments to the Secretary-General as the head of the UN Secretariat. In turn, each executive head of a UN system body makes regular program and financial reports to their governing body, demonstrating that the governing body is in principle in charge of all the secretariat activities.

In practice, the legal dependence of the secretariats on their intergovernmental body is tempered with pragmatic realities. The secretariat staff work throughout the year while the supervisory intergovernmental body may meet only once a year. Further, secretariat staff can independently solicit extra-budgetary funding for projects without prior approval of their intergovernmental supervisors; they can solicit advice from TNCs, CSOs, and other non-state actors; and participate in multistakeholder governance arrangements. UN system secretariats also have a long-standing practice to use the UN's publicly accepted neutrality – its "good offices" – to convene meetings of multi-constituency groups, including convening constituencies considered antagonistic to each other. Finally, the secretariat is seen on a daily basis by significant segments of the international community as the spokes-organization for their given topic. This dynamic indicates that some multilateral secretariats have garnered near independent status as actors in the field of global governance, even if for legal and political reasons they tend to disavow this level of autonomy in international relations.

Multilateralism and non-state actors

Non-state actors in multilateralism are those organizations which have chosen to engage with the UN system bodies and are seen by governments as having little or only a tangential dependence on any other government.

Non-state actors include for-profit or non-profit entities, scholarly institutions or high school student associations, religious bodies or atheist communities, organizations that are authoritarian or organizations that support anarchy, legally registered entities or liberation movements, for-profit organizations with hundreds of affiliates and for-profit organizations with a handful of employees, social communities or armed insurrectionists, international traditional journalist bodies or social media participants and even sometimes single individuals. For multilateralism, what connects this very broad collection of non-state actors is that they see governments as the decision-makers in international affairs and that they see their job as influencing the actions of these decision-makers. As a step in getting this job done, some non-state actors lobby secretariats in order to impact the way the secretariat frames an issue to intergovernmental bodies or the way that the secretariat staff may quietly advise individual government delegates. The characteristics of two of these non-state actors and their relationship with governments and multilateralism are examined below.

Non-governmental organizations/civil society organizations

NGOs, CSOs and social movements provide a channel for building alliances around issues and advocating for concerned communities. They often succeed in re-directing government policies, re-orienting the international dialogue, and defining new areas for the international community to address. CSOs have a powerful track record of tackling problems created by TNCs, religious bodies, the media, and the financial system. Some of these powerful institutions, which may have caused or exacerbated global problems, have discovered benefits in working with social movement organizations and CSOs. In a sense, each side of the relationship seeks to influence the other, all the while recognizing that governments are the formal decision-makers in global affairs.

As John West (2006: 154) says:

> The universe of CSOs is vast and heterogeneous, and includes (a) small, close-knit village organisations in developing countries; (b) humanitarian and emergency relief organisations, sometimes financed by governments; (c) "watchdogs" and independent monitors of government activities; (d) actors in development projects – a growing amount of official development assistance is now directed to CSOs for project implementation in developing countries; (e) environmental and human rights activism; (f) policy analysts and lobbyists; and (g) global communities of interest. (Bullets in original replaced by letters.)

Some of the humanitarian and emergency relief CSOs are also effectively consulting houses, providing project delivery for bilateral agencies and multilateral organizations. As intermediaries between donor governments and the UN system with local governments and communities, they have developed a practical working knowledge of governance and donor agency authority.

There are also overtly political CSOs or social movements whose core activity is to challenge the authority of a particular government, or more broadly a type of government or economic or social system (e.g., western capitalism or a theocratic state). Some argue that organizations that seek to overthrow a government, or that are associated with paramilitary forces, should be excluded from civil society, a criterion not used to determine if a nation-state is a legitimate member of the multilateral world. As these CSOs are challenging the dominant paradigm or are struggling to break an oppressive regime, they tend to have strong views about if and how to engage with the multilateral system.

Civil society is a really contentious place with thousands of different voices, each reaching out with their own perspectives and each organizing around different approaches to community concerns or different aspects of a person's identity (Clifford 2007). The degree of competition within the CSO world is often under-appreciated. There is competition for members, for political visibility, for access to donors, and for the acceptance of different strategic and tactical choices. This basic competitive inter-organizational reality is reflected in the difficulties that CSOs have in formulating common policy positions when engaging with intergovernmental bodies. This competition is partially managed by the multilateral process, where governments and the international secretariats can opt to open the door – or close the door – to different competing CSOs. One element of this management tool kit is the decisions on which organizations and individuals may have their travel expenses covered to attend intergovernmental meetings.

Some parts of the UN system have devised semi-permanent structures to institutionalize the interface of governments and their secretariat with non-state actors. Contemporary examples of these innovative institutional arrangements include the FAO Committee on Food Security (McKeon 2015), the role of Major Groups with the UN High-Level Political Forum on Sustainable Development, the Arria Formula for non-state participation in the Security Council (Paul 2003), and the annually scheduled BWI consultations with CSOs. UN system bodies also contract with individuals and organizations as consultants, convene high-level panels with CSO spokespersons on complex topics, and grant CSOs speaking rights at intergovernmental meetings. Building on this history, the Cardoso Commission formally proposed to create a special high-level office in the UN to regularize and strengthen the UN and governments in interacting with civil society and other non-state actors (UN 2004).

In the intergovernmental standard-setting sphere, CSOs have often campaigned for governments to fix a governance gap that allows TNCs and others in the international market to behave in ways that are legally or administratively restricted or prohibited in their home domestic markets. Through educational and media campaigns, CSOs have prompted the multilateral system to tackle a range of issues from the marketing of infant formula to the international disposal of hazardous waste. Once the CSOs have created the "political will" at the intergovernmental level, CSO experts have joined with others from national governments and secretariats in drafting detailed standards intended to remove unacceptable practices from specialized international markets. While some successes have been achieved, governments and the UN system have resisted setting ethical, health, or environmental guidelines or standards for the hundreds of thousands of products on the international market.

In many regions with armed conflicts, CSOs have played a leading role in bringing human rights issues into the debates of the Security Council. CSOs have also engaged in private diplomacy, public protection of civilians in violent areas, and extending support to migrants fleeing zones of military, environmental or economic instability. In these roles, CSOs often have functioned as partial-states, providing vital needs to a substantial number of disenfranchised citizens.

The private sector and multilateralism

While often presented as a coherent concept, the private sector is also not homogenous. The size of the business, the sector of the enterprise, and the degree of international market engagement of a given firm or sector all influence the potential role of a firm in global governance. Size is relevant, as small and medium enterprises, micro-enterprises, and mom-and-pop stores cannot be considered the same as an investment bank, a manufacturing TNC, or a global law service firm. The sector is relevant, as a manufacturing TNC, a service firm, a holding company, and a banking institution all expect and need something quite different from globalization. And international market structure is relevant, as each firm has a different perspective on global issues depending on their location along the production to consumption chain.

Since the earliest multinationals appeared on the political horizon, TNCs have operated in the international market without a state-like constraining force. At the formal intergovernmental level, TNCs have not recognized an obligation to follow inter-state decisions or declarations (Clapham 2010). If TNCs are just passive non-participants, an intergovernmental declaration may be just words on a piece of paper. In this sense, TNCs may well have the "final vote" on an intergovernmental outcome as they can obstruct – actively or passively – its implementation. The US Joint Intelligence Agency report put this in a slightly different fashion, whereby

62 *Global actors*

"... **Power is also shifting toward nonstate actors,** be they agents or spoilers of cooperation" (Commission on Global Security, Justice & Governance 2015: iv; bold in the original).

TNCs are and have always been crucial actors in global governance (WEF 2010). Most of the international economic and political space is largely governed by the firms in a given sector or geographic region (Cutler et al. 1999; May 2015). Multinational enterprises make an enormous number of decisions that affect the distribution of vital needs (e.g., the prices and quantities of food supplies) and payments for labor (e.g., the push to drive wages down between different jurisdictions); determine what products are traded in the market (e.g., the selection of products to manufacture and who can license them); and benefit from de facto local governance arrangements (e.g., export processing zones). In this sense, TNCs have de facto control over the daily needs of billions of people as well as effective control of global financial assets and cutting-edge technologies.

As explained in Chapter 2, the formal participation of the private sector in multilateralism is a recent phenomenon. Generally since WWII, TNCs have allowed OECD governments to express their views. In this role OECD governments have acted to block the UN's articulation of global standards that might be used by other governments to establish domestic practices and policies and to reject a range of possible conventions enforceable by hard law.

The exception to this relative corporate disengagement with the UN system involves the relationship between TNCs and the IMF, the World Bank, the WTO, and the World Intellectual Property Organization. Here TNCs worked directly with governments when these organizations were negotiating economic agreements on trade, finance, intellectual property rights, and development. Under the leadership of these organizations, OECD governments arranged for them to further push governments, particularly in the global South and the former socialist countries, to adopt domestic capitalist-oriented market systems.

A second exception to the minimal involvement with the UN system was when there were specific actions that could impact the business strategies of individual sectors or firms.[11] Until the 1980s, the non-economic bodies of the UN system were not seen even as particularly useful to TNCs in helping them expand business opportunities, protect their investments, or engage in inter-corporate rivalries. As noted in Chapter 1, individual parts of the UN system and OECD governments then began creating partnerships with selected TNCs. These public-private partnerships are early forms of multistakeholder governance. Under multilateralism, these project-oriented arrangements between TNCs, government agencies, local enterprises, community organizations, international CSOs, and other bodies provided a way for TNCs to "solve" market problems, particularly in areas with relatively weak public authorities. From a governance perspective, these PPPs represent the first institutional arrangement to shift power over the delivery of a public good from the nation-state to a consortium of actors led by TNCs.

Some TNCs and elite corporate bodies have also come to recognize that there are global threats so great that they cannot be managed by globalization alone. These TNCs have worked with the United Nations Framework Convention on Climate Change (UNFCCC) on mitigating climate change, with the Security Council on the economic-social recovery of former conflict zones, and with the Financial Stability Board on the stabilization of the global finance system.

New actors in multistakeholder governance

National democracies take great care in drawing election boundaries. People on one side of a street or on different sides of a river bank are declared to be in different election districts. In multistakeholderism, the current boundaries around a given stakeholder category are inherently unsettled. For example, a female Bangladeshi garment worker could be in one of three or more international governance categories in addition to being "represented" by the Bangladeshi Government and potentially by her municipal and regional governments. Without clarity on the boundaries of any given category, or clarity on how to define overlapping boundaries of categories, it is nearly impossible to judge if a particular multistakeholder governance group has a democratic foundation for legitimacy.

Transition process from multilateralism to multistakeholderism

Chapter 2 showed that the transition from multilateralism to multistakeholderism, as with any major governance or economic change, has not happened overnight. In a similar fashion, the transition in the role of global governors is an uneven process. In one part of the global standard-setting world, participants are self-consciously aiming to re-fashion specialized global markets by incorporating social, economic, and environmental standards, matters that the multilateral system effectively rejected as unacceptable governance activities. In the other part of the global standard-setting world, high-impact technology standard-setting organizations are marginalizing government involvement and the seventy-year-old multistakeholder ISO that has thrived under multilateralism. In the policy-making multistakeholder world, the transition has been less self-conscious, with key individual actors from all categories under-playing their transitions from multilateral advocates to global governors. Many of these participants have largely kept a foot in both the multilateral and the multistakeholder world.

One major element of the transition for these global leaders is learning to work with a heterogeneous group of organizations, some that were – or are still – institutional opponents. The differences in types of power external to an MSG create a fundamental asymmetry of power within the group. Challenges for multistakeholderism include how to trust other participants, how to develop shared goals, how to manage internal power imbalances, and how to accommodate diverse institutional working styles (Hemmati et al. 2002).

The shift from viewing other actors in an institutionally competitive light to recognition of a potential collaborative partnership is a difficult endeavor, and a challenge undertaken only by selected members of each competitive stakeholder group. Some participants have asserted that there is no change in their policy-making activities as under multilateralism, as that they are just continuing in their role as advocates, knowledge experts, or lobbyists but now working directly with the relevant powerful actors without the interference of governments. Other participants see themselves engaged in more "off-the-record" brainstorming sessions or Chatham House seminars, without consciously recognizing the de facto global governance functions their encounters represent. While most members of each stakeholder category remain on the sidelines, a minority of stakeholders in each are becoming governance explorers. They are looking for ways that their institutionally competitive organizations might find the appropriate political-economic space to cooperate on issues that they perceive as undermanaged or un-attended to by traditional nation-states and the UN system. The principle of volunteerism in multistakeholder governance allows certain governance explorers to drop out of a given process and move back into the broader community of organizations, watching multistakeholderism from the sidelines.

Over time, participants in the multistakeholder governance system are likely to re-align their self-perception and their political profiles to recognize the change in their international governance functions. Government officials will need to strike a balance between their legal, formal status as the core actors in global governance to one where they are just one participant in a multi-centered governance system (Slaughter 2017). For corporate executives the change includes ceasing to pretend that they do not currently have an ad hoc global governance function and acknowledging their formal leadership role in global governance. Civil society leaders will now need to transition from simply being advisors or advocates to governments or campaigners against TNCs and other powerful institutions to recognizing that they have a responsibility for the consequences on the wider community of their involvement in multistakeholderism. For UN system staff, the transition entails a shift, from where previously they largely focused on implementing the directions of an intergovernmental body, to a status where they act more independently in global governance, relying for political guidance on other more senior UN staff members.

These changes in self-perception will influence the perceptions of those situated outside MSGs. Members of the international community will no longer see CSOs as just potential advocates for a particular view or as experts on a given subject, but also as potential global governors in their own rights. Similarly, non-participants in MSGs will come to understand others participating in multistakeholder governance in a markedly different fashion.

A new governance role: the convener

Conveners of a multistakeholder arrangement now have a lead role in selecting the relevant stakeholders, defining the scope of the MSG, and proposing the operating practices for the group.[12] The convener, or someone recommended by the convener, may evolve into the facilitator of the multistakeholder governance project once it becomes a functioning organization. The convener function may be led by a single dominant organization, two or more organizations working closely together from one or more different stakeholder categories, or an intergovernmental secretariat body acting on its own or with intergovernmental authority. For example, the organizational conveners of the Marine Stewardship Council were Unilever and the WWF; of the World Commission on Dams, the World Bank and the IUCN; of The Alliance for Affordable Internet, Google and USAID; and of the Global Mining Initiative, the World Business Council of Sustainable Development (WBSCD) and the International Institute for Education and Development (IIED). As is the case with high-impact technology standard-setting bodies, there can be contested claims to the role of convener.

In a multilateral world, the role of gatekeeper and guard of legitimacy in global affairs is performed by the nation-state, working with other nation-states directly or collectively through the UN system. In a multistakeholder world, the convener takes on this gatekeeping function to global decision-making, while aspiring to build sufficient legitimacy for the particular multistakeholder project that it can exercise effective authority. The largely unrestrained power of the convener means that it is difficult to sustain a claim to democratic legitimacy for multistakeholderism in global governance.

Adam et al. (2007: 16–17) describe the convener role in this manner:

> A multi-stakeholder process for ... policy begins with a champion organisation identifying a policy issue.... A champion in this case would be an individual or organisation that is trusted and respected by all stakeholders and plays a catalytic role throughout the engagement process. The champion identifies potential participants and sets the multi-stakeholder process in motion.

One of the early decisions made by the convener is the choice of the appropriate collection of multistakeholder categories that are required for a new group. The convener is almost certainly going to ensure that the group has actors which, in the mind of the convener, are most likely to be able to make changes happen. The convener could also assign priorities to organizations that have recently expressed interest in a given crisis or situation, those who may be able to garner the best publicity on the issue, those who might bring political or technical expertise to the table, those associated with potential funding sources or those who may be most affected by the potential outcomes of the multistakeholder process.

Table 3.1 illustrates the variety of stakeholder categories that thirteen different conveners utilized to balance the stakeholder categories participating in a multistakeholder project. Conveners cited in this table elected to bring on board anywhere from four to fifteen different stakeholder categories. In each of these particular examples, the convener could have easily expanded each discrete category to be more inclusive (examples appear in parentheses in the final column) or collapsed categories to reduce the number of actors. In each example, note the relative distribution of categories between the different types of perspectives that the convener used and the relevant under-representation of stakeholder categories that might be most affected by the potential actions of the MSG. What is not at all clear, however, is whether the democratic status of the group is enhanced by expanding the number of sub-categories or undermined by compacting categories.

Even these stakeholder categories are not unambiguous. The government stakeholder category may mean the national, a state/provincial, or a municipal government, a parliamentary body, or part of the judicial court system. Similarly, the academic category could include any one of a number of difference disciplines, professional associations, or university administrators. For additional examples on the ambiguity in stakeholder categories, see Table 3.2 below.

Often, the convener chooses to narrow down the relevant categories of stakeholders into what the convener feels is a "manageable" or "preferred" size. This managerial push toward smaller sized governing bodies may well run counter to ensuring that all actors who have a stake are involved. Stakeholder governing bodies tend to range in size from five to twenty-five. By way of contrast, getting a representative balance in OECD democracies involves parliaments ranging in size from the mid-100s in New Zealand to over 600 in the UK and Germany (Jacobs and Otjes 2014).

Conveners of MSGs can winnow down categories by selecting the most economically or politically powerful categories – without this group "nothing can be done" – and by providing a limited number of categories for all other potential actors. Alternatively, they can aggregate categories of a "similar" type. A CSO category could be said to represent academics, media, and religious bodies as well as the more obvious social movement category. One or two designees in the "business" category could be said to "represent" all types of commercial actors irrespective of their size,

Table 3.1 Examples related to the diversity of categories of stakeholders

Name of multistakeholder group	Scope of activity	Current categories and possible other relevant categories (in parentheses)
Global Reporting Initiative	International standards for environmental and socioeconomic sustainability	Business, labor, civil society, mediating institutions (Government, scientific expertise, international organizations, pension funds)
The Factories of the Future	Manufacturing research and innovation	Manufacturers in automotive, aerospace, engineering, suppliers, service providers, academic and research institutes and regional and national innovation clusters (Other high technology industrial sectors, specialist manufacturers)
Hydropower Sustainability Assessment Protocol	Promotes and guides hydropower projects	Governments, civil society, financial institutions and the hydropower sector (Upstream communities, downstream agricultural producers)
Natural Capital Coalition	Conservation of natural capital	Organizations from research, science, academia, business, advisory, membership, accountants, reporting, standard-setting, finance, investment, policy, government, conservation and civil society (Corporate chief financial officers [CFOs,] socially responsible investor [SRI] standard setters, critics of monetarizing nature, real estate assessors)
Better Biomass	Biomass certification scheme	Producers, processors, traders, end users, non-governmental organizations, research institutions, government/authorities, conformity assessment bodies, service providers (Other alternative energy suppliers, forest stewardship organizations, indigenous peoples organizations)

Source: The author.

Table 3.2 Potential stakeholder categories for a multistakeholder-based governance system

Category	Selected sub-divisions
Governments	At the national, regional, and municipal levels; from parliaments to heads of state offices
Civil society organizations	At the international, regional and national levels; social movements, development, humanitarian, and environmental NGOs
Academics	From philosophers to physicists to professors of religion
Gender-based	Women's rights organizations or lesbian, gay, bisexual and transgender (LGBT) rights movements
Human rights groups	From legal advocates to social movements seeking redress for human rights violations
Investors	From insurance firms to venture capital funds; from philanthropy investors to social impact investors
Manufacturing and servicing firms	From multinational corporations to medium-sized national enterprises to small and micro local businesses; from minority-owned businesses to green global enterprises
Advocates for thematic challenges	Such as spokespersons for the hunger crisis, the poverty crisis, future generations, and the ecological crisis
Religious bodies	From the centrally structured Catholic Church to autonomous ethical bodies
Non-state development groups	Such as Oxfam, World Resources Institute (WRI), Doctors without Borders, and international development volunteers
Indigenous peoples	From different continents or from different international federations
Labor organizations	From international confederations of trade unions to sector-based national trade unions to autonomous groups of workers
Trade and professional associations	Such as the International Chamber of Commerce (ICC), the International Accounting Standards Board (IASB), and the International Association of Agricultural Economists
UN system bodies	Such as the FAO, United Nations University (UNU), and the International Fund for Agricultural Development (IFAD)
Rio's nine Major Groups	Such as local governments and youth (see Table 3.3 for additional details)
Independent individuals	Such as educators, senior citizens, or nearby residents and communities, celebrities, and retired public officials

Source: The author.

geographic location, or type of economic sector. The variety of convener and founder choices, which can range from four stakeholder categories to eleven stakeholder categories, is presented in Table 3.3.

When the convener is a TNC or a government actor, they may well select those categories of stakeholders that are more likely to be supportive of the convener's preference in regard to the expected outcome of the group. This means that categories of stakeholders that are not seen by the sponsors as potentially cooperative – particularly those groups that will be negatively affected by the likely outcome of the MSG – are generally excluded from the start of the process. As the boundaries between stakeholder categories and the number of different stakeholder categories in a given stakeholder group are not governed by informal or formal standards, the convener's choice defines and controls the process from the very beginning.

Adam et al. (2007: 14) also argue that:

> The multi-stakeholder process has to ensure that all relevant stakeholders are included. Participants should feel that they are treated equally in discussing the issues under consideration. This is particularly important when various parties may come into the process with unequal power bases.

The concern for balancing unequal power, which may not be shared by all conveners, is a major democratic challenge for multistakeholderism. In the current arrangements for MSGs, there is no institutional mechanism to ensure that the convener's selection of stakeholder members reflects geographic balance, gender balance, worker inclusion, communities most likely to be affected by the actions of the group, or the participation of organizations and individuals at the bottom end of the global social structure. Designating a person to participate in the MSG from one of the under-represented communities does not solve the challenge. Having one token woman or one member of the Southern community among twelve men or an equal number of international experts can easily mean that, while there is a minimum presence, that voice is dwarfed by the unbalanced weight of the entire MSG.

The flexibility in the coverage of a category can lead to internal confusions inside a given MSG and significant misconceptions external to the group. Internally, some stakeholder may look at others and assume they cover a wider range of communities and stakeholders than the actual participant perceives about their own role in the process. Individuals and organizations outside the MSG may look at the legitimacy of the undertaking with a high degree of suspicion if they don't see what they take to be their constituent category explicitly engaged in the process. This winnowing process, while it has some clear organizational and efficiency benefits, may well open the multistakeholder group to critiques about fairness and legitimacy, hampering its own consensus-building process.

Table 3.3 Diversity of the number of categories of stakeholders in a multistakeholder governance group

Organization	Number of categories	Titles of stakeholder categories and number of organizations in each category, if specified
Ethical Trade Initiative	4	Global companies, international trade union bodies, specialized labor rights organizations, and development charities
Alliance for Affordable Internet	4	Global sponsors (2); private sector (11); public sector/academia (25); civil society/foundations (28)
Construction Sector Transparency Initiative	5	Civil society (2); government (1); industry (1), university (1); consultant (1)
Global Network Initiative	5	Companies (10); NGOs (5); academics (2); investors community (2); independent chair (1)
World Economic Forum's New Vision for Agriculture Initiative	6	Government; private sector; farmers; civil society; donors/international organizations; research/thought leaders
International Union for Conservation of Nature	6	Framework Partners (8); government partners (35); multilateral institutions (21); NGOs (16); foundations (29); companies and corporate foundations (1)
Roll Back Malaria	6	Malaria-affected countries; bilateral and multilateral development partners; private sector; non-governmental and community-based organizations; philanthropic foundations; research and academic institutions
Golf Environmental Organization	6	Strategic global partners (3); industry associations (16); national partners (10); corporate partners (5); environment and research (8); recognized service providers (3)
Global Sustainable Tourism Council	8	Industry (5), NGOs (5), trade associations (2), senior staff (2), academic (1), UN system (1), public authority (1), certification body (1)
Major Groups	9	Women, children and youth, farmers, local authorities, business, trade unions, scientific and technological community, indigenous people, non-governmental organizations

Global actors 71

Table 3.3 Continued

Organization	Number of categories	Titles of stakeholder categories and number of organizations in each category, if specified
GAVI: The Vaccine Alliance	11	Independent individuals (9); developing country governments (6); donor governments (5); Bill & Melinda Gates Foundation (1); WHO (1); UNICEF (1); World Bank (1); research and technical health institutes (1); vaccine industry developing countries (1); vaccine industry developed countries (1); civil society (1); the Chief Executive Officer of GAVI

Sources: WHO 2016; Ethical Trading Initiative n.d.; Alliance for Affordable Internet n.d.; Nelson and Jenkins 2016; IUCN n.d.; RBM 2016.

For project-oriented MSGs, the convener and other leading participants have an additional criterion. Whether the project-oriented group is a PPP with a geographic and time-bound scope or an international project-oriented MSG with a longer-term horizon, the individual from each organization has to have sufficient authority within their institution to deliver on their commitments. If a TNC sends a member of their external relations group or a government asks a junior member of the department to attend, then the implementation capacity of the project-oriented group can be severely constrained. On the other hand, if the CEO, Minister, or similarly ranked individual from other stakeholder categories is a member of the project-oriented group, there is a high likelihood that that official will not have sufficient time to regularly participate in a project-focused MSG.

Changed role for state actors in the new global governance system

In multilateralism, governments are not only in the room, they are in the chair, they are members of the intergovernmental coordinating bureau, and they are the ones who can vote. They can elect to participate in all meetings of the international organizations of which they are members. Under multistakeholderism, in contrast, the choice is no longer in government hands. The convener of an MSG is often the one that selects which governments are invited to participate and which governments are not. As conveners tend to come from institutions of the North, there is a likelihood that the selection of government participants will be biased against governments from the South and particularly against governments from smaller developing countries.

In the multilateral system, a government's position is generally coordinated by a single national ministry or department. In multistakeholderism, it is not clear if governments as institutions are even invited into the new global governance room, and, if so, who a government official represents. Is the *government delegate*, if this is still the appropriate term, participating on behalf of their individual national government, on behalf of a group of geopolitically similar states, on behalf of the official's agency, on behalf of a given province/state, on behalf of a specific municipality? As noted earlier, some sub-national government units are being granted semi-formal international status in negotiations without having to deal with their parallel units at home or their national authorities. In addition to the surrender of exclusive power in formal international decision-making, the ambiguity about the status of the government person in the room indicates how significant the shift is for governments with the advent of multistakeholderism.

Looked at from the bottom up, the changed role for nation-state actors is even more complicated. If one subtracts all the members of the other stakeholder groups participating in a given MSG, what fraction of the domestic citizenry is left unrepresented? In representation terms, the *government delegate* may then be a residual stakeholder. In this case, how should the other members of the MSG understand the government delegate's "stake" in the MSG mission? One alternative explanation is that the government delegate is not a residual stakeholder but is invited into an MSG to co-opt the old order into an acceptance of multistakeholderism, or to provide access to funding, legal status and military authority.

Some major MSGs have established rules and institutional arrangements to keep governments an arm's-length away from their decision-making bodies. ICANN, for example, has a governance structure where governments and intergovernmental organizations are only one of a number of advisory bodies (ICANN n.d.). The Global Reporting Initiative, which gained international prominence through UNEP's early involvement, had a simpler exclusion approach; it eliminated any role for governments or the UN system in its on-going governance structure (GRI n.d.).

Standard-setting MSGs also tend to exclude governments from their decision-making process. In part, the exclusion derives from their founding rationale: autonomous standard-setting groups were created because governments chose not to set global market standards that were customer/worker/environmentally meaningful. In some cases, bilateral agencies, which are significant funders of a particular standard-setting body, are invited to take on leadership of the group.

International project-oriented MSGs represent one of the clearest changes in the role of governments in international public affairs. In multilateralism, intergovernmental bodies can adopt resolutions containing global soft law statements as well as follow-up assignments to their secretariat. Under multistakeholderism, however, global project-oriented and policy-oriented MSGs tend to publicize their actions as steps taken in accordance with goals and targets set by the intergovernmental bodies of the UN system. As multistakeholder bodies are under no direct obligation to report to the original intergovernmental body, there is no effective way for an intergovernmental organization to alter their implementation plan or to disavow the public assertions about the degree of commitment of the MSG to the intergovernmental resolution.

Further, were the intergovernmental body to adopt a revised statement of goals or a new plan of action, the MSG would not be under any direct obligation to follow the revised statement. The transfer of authority from the UN system to an MSG significantly weakens governmental authority in the international sphere. This transformation of authority in governance is similar to that which has occurred in PPPs. By surrendering the oversight of the implementation to a multistakeholder body, governments have given the multistakeholder participants political space to re-fashion international goals and targets in their own interests. By the early 2000s, the transformation in the role of intergovernmental processes with multistakeholder implementation was regarded as the new normal. The 2002 Hague Conference of the Parties to the Convention on Biodiversity and the 2015 Paris Conference of the Parties to the UNFCCC adopted intergovernmental statements which appealed for multistakeholders to take the lead in the implementation of their intergovernmental decisions.

Governments under multistakeholderism have significantly shifted global decision-making power to other stakeholders or have stepped back as other international actors have asserted a global leadership role. What is less clear is what is happening with the prior assignment of responsibilities, obligations, and liabilities held by nation-states that were developed under the Westphalian model. If a degree of responsibility, obligation, and liability are not now transferred to the international body acting as a governance institution, is the democratic process of accountability reduced proportionally? Clarity on this potential transfer of legal burdens remains to be determined by practice and court decisions in the coming years.

Changed role of the UN system secretariats as independent actors in global governance

In multilateralism, international secretariats receive their authority from an intergovernmental body. Under multistakeholderism, they can maintain that status, while having a distinct role in global governance by creating or joining an MSG without meaningful supervision from any intergovernmental body.

The change from the UN system's traditional convener role is also significant. In the multistakeholder world, a UN system secretariat may now host a semi-permanent multistakeholder body, like the Global Compact, which in its early years explicitly avoided intergovernmental authorization.[13] The UN Secretary-General's office also created on its own authority a series of high-level corporate and financial bodies to influence the flow of capital in specific economic and social sectors.[14] Multistakeholder bodies established or managed by international organizations provide the MSG with a degree of public legitimacy derived from the parent UN system body.

UN secretariats can be invited by a convener to participate in an MSG hosted outside of the intergovernmental system. UN staff can be seen by the convener and other members of the MSG both as substantive experts and as transmission links to governments and UN agencies. The UN system, however, has no formal procedure for pre-approval of any invitation to participate in an external multistakeholder body and no pre-approval or post-approval system for what UN system staff may advocate or approve within any given MSG.[15]

These secretariat changes are significant from a governance perspective in that the fundamental role of the secretariat has been to support intergovernmental bodies and implement their programs. With the advent of multistakeholderism, the secretariats have gained greater autonomy as independent actors in global governance and can hold an equivalently comfortable seat at the table with any government, acting formally as an intergovernmental supervisor.

Changed role for civil society organizations in global governance

While some CSOs have decided to be involved with MSGs, others have elected not to be involved. Some CSOs opt to keep open the opportunity to engage with governments under multilateral rules and practices while they also participate in MSGs. As global standard-setting MSGs and PPPs can function for a number of years, some CSOs are forced to make an explicit choice about their participation in multistakeholderism. They can accept an invitation to participate in a standard-setting MSG or they can decline an invitation and sacrifice any ability to set the rules or practices in a given area.

The study by the Global Redesign Initiative (GRI) concluded that there are three new governance roles for CSOs in multistakeholderism. First, senior CSO leaders can be effective teachers to TNC executives about the social and economic challenges in the world, particularly those challenges that flow from globalization into developing countries. This educational function is considered necessary by the WEF, as senior corporate executives have highly developed knowledge about their particular global market segments and its interconnections with related international markets, but they are less well educated about broader social and economic realities. The second function is to act as a moral compass for TNC executives. Private executives have one key moral imperative – to meet a profit and loss standard and to manage corporate assets and liabilities in the best possible way for the firm and its stockholders. Becoming an effective global governor means that TNC leaders will need to significantly broaden their normal moral objectives. The third function is to transmit to national and local CSOs the views and concerns of TNCs and the governing MSG.

Not all CSOs have an equal chance to be invited to join an MSG. Some international CSOs are stable, long-standing institutions. These tend to have better access to the resources to participate in international events, they have the institutional capacity to maintain a long-term commitment to the engagement process, and they are better known to the conveners of MSGs (Utting 2002). Most CSOs however are not in this category. Developing country CSOs and CSOs from other economically weaker regions, for example, can participate only if other institutions cover their basic participation costs. In addition, some potential CSO participants are so focused on challenging global systemic issues that their opportunity to be invited inside an MSG is sharply limited.

Besides this organizational bias, there is no clear way to assign a representative category to a concept or to a specific non-human constituency. As noted earlier, global social, economic, gender, or environmental concepts and the realities they are associated with are simply not unambiguous in character; they are complex in their own right and in their interactions with each other. In spite of these difficulties – or maybe because of them – some proponents of representing these categories ignore complex issues of representativeness and assert that minimal representation of a particular, albeit undefined category, is more positive than no participation whatsoever. Ambiguities about the boundaries of categories take on a new meaning when those categories are used in global governance institutions. The convener has the power to decide which competitive CSOs will be designated to represent what civil society concerns and which other CSOs are excluded from the process.

For CSOs invited into the multistakeholder world, it signifies potentially a major change in status – one extended by the convener of a particular MSG rather than by the CSO's peer community. For project delivery CSOs, the major change is moving from acting as an intermediary in delivering a public good to becoming a project designer and overseer in conjunction with state and commercial institutions that may well have caused – or may well benefit from – a particular project. For CSOs involved in environmental and social standard-setting bodies, they are now confronted with managing conflicting intra-corporate demands in setting the floor for their standards and the global competition for acceptance of their certified product classifications. In this latter case, these CSOs in their home countries would argue for the primacy of science-based regulatory decisions and oppose environmental and social standards being developed with any overt attention to the costs for the private sector.

The change in status may also mean a change in global responsibilities. What if the standard for the product is inadequately certified and the credibility of a developing country's niche product market and its income collapses? What if a multistakeholder project elicits an adverse reaction from a key local community? What if an MSG advances a market-based policy solution that has unintended consequences for marginal or migrant communities?

As discussed in Chapter 2, changes in CSO relations with the UN system evolved in parallel with changes in the private sector relationship with the UN system.

Changed role of private sector actors in global governance

For most TNCs, the dominant reality in a multistakeholder world remains that the UN system is marginal to their business interests.[16] TNCs will continue to compete with other TNCs to exert global control over access to natural resources, markets, technologies, workers, and the flow of capital. In commercial market terms, multistakeholderism provides a new way to create global markets for products directed at environmentally and socially concerned consumers. It is also a new way to develop stable global markets for high-impact technologies without obligatory public hearings and government oversight.

Those TNCs that participate in standard-setting MSGs know they can use that process to aid market expansion by establishing the standards that a growing niche of the world's consumers find beneficial. At the same time, they can use their participation to leverage their ability to address under-managed aspects of the global ecology, which if left under-regulated, may well be disruptive to globalization. Once again, the democratic challenge here rests on the clear conflict of interest involved. In partnering with selected CSOs and professional specialists in a given niche market, individual TNC participants can both expand their market share against other potential competitors and define the scope of acceptable social/economic/environmental standards in particular global markets, a practice that in OECD countries is usually reserved for the nation-state.

For other TNCs or divisions of TNCs, there are multiple structural rationales to supplement these commercial benefits. On one level, some TNC executives recognize that they need to take dramatic steps to stabilize the globalization project, particularly after the 2008/2009 Global Recession and the increase in potential instability from adverse changes in the levels of global inequality. A second rationale for some TNCs follows from an understanding that without some enhanced public engagement, there is a likelihood that market-based solutions may become delegitimized over time. A third rationale is the recognition that some of the challenges facing the globalization project, such as planet-wide ecological shifts, capital market instabilities, and the social consequences of some advanced technologies, lie so far outside the capacity of national governments to address them, and are so crucial for the long-term survival of the capitalist market system, that TNCs need to join with other actors to develop a quasi-state intervention to attempt to manage these crises. One of the key MSGs implementing this rationale is the World Economic Forum's Network of Global Future Councils.[17] This network brings together 20–30 key individuals from the corporate world, the academic world, government world, and civil society into a series of 40–60 work groups to formulate global policy directions for cutting-edge global crises.

The GRI study acknowledged a number of limitations to the formal switch for TNCs from multilateralism to multistakeholderism. TNC executives are, by training and due to their reward structures, primarily focused on increasing income or reducing costs for their individual firm. This frame of mind and the associated financial self-interest does not, in WEF's understanding, make for a good global governor who has to grasp a far wider view of globalization than one based on a specific product or service. Global governors also have to be able to partially set aside short-termism and make broad moral judgements. To address the lack of a sound corporate moral compass, the GRI proposes that all corporate executives take a new Hippocratic Oath as a step toward learning how to be effective as public global governors (WEF 2010: 52).

TNCs are discovering that participating in policy-oriented MSGs, such as Investors for Climate Change, gives them an opportunity to expand their understanding of global and regional problems while meeting senior officials, which may also aid them in traditional ways with their own corporate marketing and expansion plans. This latter function, similar to that which exists under multilateralism, opens a number of very significant conflict of interest concerns. Moreover, giving commercial actors a public role in decision-making or a private venue to engage with decision-makers that impacts their own businesses is as problematic on the domestic level as it is on the international level. As noted in Chapter 1, the definition of conflict of interest in the international domain is even more complex than it is in current OECD country practice.

TNCs actively participating in PPPs will see little change between their current practices and what their functions were in the multilateral world. What will change will be the role of TNCs in international project-oriented MSGs and in policy-making MSGs. The challenge for senior corporate executives is thus two-fold. First, TNCs will need to learn how to manage public expectations that MSGs including TNCs will be able to deliver the goals adopted by UN system bodies. Second, TNCs will need to accommodate themselves to public claims of responsibility and liabilities for any perceived failure from the outcome of a given MSG.

These initiatives are not undertaken by all TNCs. Even those TNCs or divisions of TNCs which have started down this path have insisted that all these new interventions are voluntary. Individual TNCs can thus step away from a particular multistakeholder project or distance themselves from multistakeholderism as a whole, whenever they feel that the directions of these activities are not to their liking.

Donors adapt to multistakeholderism

Under multilateralism, most international donor institutions – be they private foundations, bilateral agencies, or multilateral development banks – have governance structures where the donor and the donor's board of directors set the grant priorities and make grant approvals. CGIAR, the international funding system for agricultural research, is the exception. The CGIAR's System Council involves fifteen representatives from among CGIAR's funders and five developing country representatives that are either countries hosting a CGIAR Research Center, countries with significant national agricultural systems, or countries that are also CGIAR funders (CGIAR n.d.).

In the multistakeholder world, the new normal for funder-centered MSGs increasingly follows the CGIAR model. Major donors from the Bill and Melinda Gates Foundation to the UN Secretary-General's fund-raising office are creating multistakeholder governance financing structures. Whether the new multistakeholder bodies, for example GAVI and Every Women Every Child, are founded by private, largely corporate influences, or by international secretariats and governments, the funders and founders remain in control. The formal presence of a diverse group of stakeholders in the governing body, however, provides a different public reality. For GAVI-type bodies, multistakeholder funding bodies assert that the presence of diverse stakeholder constituencies on their decision-making bodies makes them more accountable and better connected with their relevant communities.

However, as there is a sharp drop in government funding to UN system bodies, this concentration of financial power outside the multilateral arena means that these donor-established multistakeholder bodies can displace intergovernmental leadership in setting internationally shared policy priorities and programs. When the international secretariat "coordinates" private financial flows through multistakeholder bodies which are dominated by private firms, the imbalance in relative power – convening power verses capital and marketing power – means that these bodies can re-define the soft law directions of international bodies while asserting that they are working under the UN system umbrella.

Other non-state actors become participants in governance under multistakeholderism

Many MSGs designate as stakeholders academics, religious leaders, retired corporate executives, celebrities, lawyers, accountants, trade unionists, local community leaders, former public officials, small business owners, sports leaders, and media spokespeople. In most of these cases, it is not clear why any single individual involved in an MSG can claim to have more of a "stake" than an average person.

Some of these stakeholders come from social institutions where there is little or no practical basis to claim a representational connection, but they are identified with that social institution in order to bring the legitimacy of their participating institutions to a given MSG. Academic stakeholders do not represent their university, nor do they represent their whole discipline, other scholarly disciplines, or even their own academic department within their university. The same could be said for members of the clergy, media personalities, sports leaders and former politicians. Former elected officials, retired senior UN system officials, movie stars, news broadcasters, and religious leaders may be recruited to MSGs without any direct or indirect claim that they can "represent" an important social institution. They are often seen as individuals with sufficient expertise and political connections to be invited for their practical wisdom or for their support in potentially generating external acceptance. In either case, the process of selectively elevating these individuals to be global governors poses complicated democratic questions. On what plausible democratic basis are these individuals introduced into an MSG? Equally, on what plausible basis should labor leaders, indigenous peoples or youth *not* be included in all MSGs?

Other individuals with professional expertise – lawyers, accountants, IT managers, and medical doctors – are also invited to be global governors based on claims of meritocracy, rather than on their claim to have a special stake in the crisis or issue. These professional skills and knowledge were previously engaged in an international project under simple professional contracts or pro bono arrangements. The designation of a particular professional to participate in a given MSG elevates one professional approach over a competing professional discipline without any opportunity for other professionals to engage equally in the global governance. As wise as these professionals may be, using convener-selected meritocracy as a stakeholder category without public review or approval is not a democratically justified criterion.

The argument presented here is that changes among the formal global decision-makers are significant in their own right, and particularly significant in assessing the democratic character of multistakeholderism. From a governance perspective, these changes should be explored properly before further acceptance of multistakeholderism gains public hold. Multistakeholderism is based also on a number of strongly held organizational beliefs and on a variety of institutional structures, which are the subject of Chapter 4.

Notes

1 The primary document today on state responsibility is the Articles on the Responsibility of States for Internationally Wrongful Acts, adopted by the International Law Commission (Borelli 2017).
2 For example, the Vienna Convention on Diplomatic Relations (1961) is an international treaty that defines diplomatic relations between countries, and the

80 *Global actors*

　　　Vienna Convention on the Law of Treaties (1969) codifies international law on treaties themselves at the international level.
3 For example, there is the Third Geneva Convention regarding the treatment of prisoners of war (last revision in 1949) and the Fourth Geneva Convention on the protections of civilians in time of war (1949).
4 In multilateralism, however, there are also institutions where this core democratic principle is by-passed in the claimed interest of key powerful nation-states. The founding documents for the Security Council, the World Bank, and the IMF, for instance, have enshrined an unequal voting system for institutions of peace and security, and international economic and monetary affairs.
5 In 1995, the institution of the GATT officially transitioned into the WTO.
6 The exception to leadership by a department of state or ministry of foreign affairs involves international engagement on finance and trade and international leadership on military matters. In the finance and trade areas, the lead nation-state office is more often the more powerful ministry of external trade/economics, or the national central bank.
7 See the ILO Constitution (1919), Article 3.
8 Other similar international standard-setting organizations, given authority by nation-states, include the association that prepares international accounting rules (the International Accounting Standards Board) and standards for electrical products (the International Electrotechnical Commission).
9 The WTO's Agreement on Technical Barriers to Trade.
10 Other similar public science bodies are the International Panel on Climate Change and the International Union of Pure and Applied Chemistry.
11 For example, the FAO pesticide standard-settings, the WHO essential medicines requirements, and the WHO rules on tobacco and breast milk substitutes.
12 As Gasser et al. (2015: 18) write,

> Although reasons for this varied, in all of [our] case studies, the conveners exercised some degree of control and discretion over the number and types of participants.... In [two cases], the significant government involvement in those governance groups meant that participants were selected for their compatibility with the policymakers involved.

13 Today, the Global Compact continues to function with only ex-post facto reporting to the UN General Assembly.
14 For example, Sustainable Energy for All (SE4All) and Every Women Every Child.
15 However, the UN leaves this determination to the individual staff member who is expected to sign a memo saying that involvement in an MSG does not interfere with their work time or cause a conflict of interest.
16 The exceptions to this general statement, noted in the earlier section, remain the same.
17 This group was originally called the "Global Agenda Council Network."

References

Abbot, Kenneth W. and Duncan Snidal. 2009. "Hard and Soft Law in International Governance." *International Organization* 54, no. 3: 421–56.
Adam, Lishan, Tina James, and Munyua Wanjira. 2007. "Frequently asked questions about multi-stakeholder partnerships in ICTs for development: A guide for national ICP policy animators." Melville, South Africa: Association for Progressive Communications.

Alliance for Affordable Internet. n.d. "Members." Accessed March 15, 2018. Available from http://a4ai.org/members/.

Borelli, Silvia. 2017. "State Responsibility in International Law." Last modified June 27, 2017. Accessed May 15, 2017. Available from www.oxfordbibliographies.com/view/document/obo-9780199796953/obo-9780199796953-0031.xml#firstMatch.

Commission on Global Security, Justice & Governance. 2015. "Confronting the Crisis of Global Governance." The Hague and Washington DC: Commission on Global Security, Justice & Governance.

CGIAR. n.d. "Governance." Accessed February 4, 2018. Available from www.cgiar.org/how-we-work/governance/.

Cutler, A. Claire, Virginia Haufler, and Tony Porter. 1999. "The Contours and Significance of Private Authority in International Affairs" in Cutler, A. Claire, Virginia Haufler, and Tony Porter (eds) *Private Authority and International Affairs*. Albany, NY: SUNY Press, 333–76.

Clapham, Andrew. 2010. Human Rights Obligations of Non-State Actors. New York: Oxford University Press.

Clifford, Bob. 2007. *The Marketing of Rebellion: Insurgents, Media, and International Activism*. New York: Cambridge University Press.

Ethical Trading Initiative. n.d. "Our members." Accessed March 15, 2018. Available from www.ethicaltrade.org/about-eti/our-members.

Gasser, Urs, Ryan Budish and Sarah West. 2015. "Multistakeholder as Governance Groups: Observations from Case Studies." Cambridge, MA: Berkman Klein Center, Harvard University.

GRI. n.d. "Board of Directors." Accessed June 15, 2017. Available from www.globalreporting.org/information/about-gri/governance-bodies/board-of-directors/Pages/default.aspx.

Hemmati, Minu, Felix Dodds, Jasmin Enayati, and Jan McHarry. 2002. *Multistakeholder Processes for Governance and Sustainability: Beyond Deadlock and Conflict*. London: Earthscan.

ICANN. n.d. "Governmental Advisory Committee." Accessed March 16, 2018. Available from https://gac.icann.org.

ILO. 1919. *Constitution of the International Labour Organisation (ILO)*, April 1, 1919. Available from www.refworld.org/docid/3ddb5391a.html.

Interim Commission for the International Trade Organization. 1948. *United Nations Conference on Trade and Employment: Final Act and Related Documents*. UN doc E/Conf. 2/78. (Held at Havana, Cuba, November 21, 1947 – March 24, 1948. Agreed Lake Success, New York. April 1948).

ISO. 2016. "ISO figures for 2016." Last modified 2016. Accessed December 27, 2017. Available from www.iso.org/iso-in-figures.html.

IUCN. n.d. "Donors and Partners." Accessed December 17, 2017. Available from www.iucn.org/about/donors-and-partners.

Jacobs, Kristof and Simon Otjes. 2014. "Explaining reforms of assembly sizes: Reassessing the cube root law relationship between population and assembly size." (Presentation, ECPR General Conference in Glasgow, Scotland, September 3–6, 2014). Available from https://ecpr.eu/Filestore/PaperProposal/3bc100be-56fe-4efc-8d8c-a1f0b85e7f24.pdf.

May, Christopher. 2015. "Who's in charge? Corporations as institutions of global governance." *Palgrave Communications* 1, article no. 15042: 1–10.

McKeon, Nora. 2015. *Food Security Governance: Empowering Communities, Regulating Corporations*. London: Routledge.

Murphy, Craig N. and Joanne Yates. 2009. *International Organization for Standardization: Global Governance Through Voluntary Consensus (Global Institutions)*, 1st Edition. New York: Routledge.

Nelson, Jane and Beth Jenkins. 2016. "Tackling Global Challenges: Lessons in System Leadership from the World Economic Forum's New Vision for Agriculture Initiative." Cambridge, MA: CSR Initiative, Harvard Kennedy School.

Paul, James. 2003. "The Arria Formula." Last modified October 2003. Global Policy Forum. Available from www.globalpolicy.org/component/content/article/185/40088.html.

RBM. 2016. "Organizational Structure." Last modified June 2016. Available from https://rollbackmalaria.com/organizational-structure/.

Slaughter, Anne-Marie. 2017. *The Chessboard and the Web: Strategies of Connection in a Networked World*. New Haven, CT: Yale University Press.

UN. 1974. *Declaration on the Establishment of a New International Economic Order*. GA Agenda Item 7, UN GA 6th Special session, UN Doc A/RES/S-6/3201 (distributed May 1, 1974).

UN. 2004. *Strengthening of the United Nations System: Note by the Secretary-General*, GA Agenda Item 59, UN GA 58th session, UN Doc A/58/817 (distributed June 11, 2004).

Utting, Peter. 2002. "Regulating Business via Multistakeholder Initiatives: A Preliminary Assessment." In Jenkins, Rhys, Peter Utting, and Renato Alva Pino (eds) *Voluntary Approaches to Corporate Readings and a Resource Guide*. Geneva: United Nations Non-Governmental Liaison Service (NGLS) and United Nations Research Institute for Social Development (UNRISD).

WEF. 2010. "Everybody's Business: Strengthening International Cooperation in a More Interdependent World: Report of the Global Redesign Initiative." Geneva: World Economic Forum.

West, John. 2006. "Multistakeholder Diplomacy at the OECD." In Kurbalija, J. and V. Katrandjiev (eds) *Multistakeholder Diplomacy: Challenges and Opportunities*. Malta: DiploFoundation, 149–63.

WHO. 2016. *Framework of Engagement with Non-State Actors*. 69th World Health Assembly, Agenda Item 11.3, WHO Doc. WHA69.10 (distributed May 28, 2016).

4 Structural and institutional characteristics of multistakeholderism

Organizational beliefs about multistakeholderism in general and about the specific institutional structures of individual multistakeholder groups have a significant impact on the democratic governance possibilities of a given multistakeholder organization.

The first part of this chapter presents a set of organizational beliefs often held by proponents of multistakeholderism and the governance consequences of these beliefs. These beliefs are shared by all three types of multistakeholder groups. From a sociological perspective, these organizational beliefs influence the daily internal operations of a multistakeholder group and affect the perspective of non-participants about the group's legitimacy. Some participants in a multistakeholder group may not be aware of these organizational beliefs and may initially argue that they are incorrect. Other participants, who have thought about these organizational beliefs, may well feel sufficiently uncomfortable with them as they may present a contradiction with their own personal political and economic beliefs. As with other organizational beliefs, they are generally not evidence-based conclusions, but rather strongly shared viewpoints by participants reflected in their writing and interviews. Some of these beliefs are closely associated with a search for democratic legitimacy; others with a desire to create a working environment that can overcome differences in work cultures and asymmetries of power.

The second part of this chapter looks at the structural characteristics of multistakeholder groups, alongside the governance consequences of particular institutional forms. At the birth of a multistakeholder project, the convener and other founding members often have a robust debate about the group's structural design. Each founding participant is reasonably focused on ensuring that the structure embodies their aspirations for the group, and that the structure has a plausible chance of reconciling conflicting interests and producing a positive end result. However, there is no standardized process – no Robert's Rules of Order – dictating how multistakeholder groups should make decisions fairly and address internal conflicts. Once the multistakeholder group begins work, the structural arrangements largely condition responses to potential external governance challenges. It is quite difficult to change the basic institutional form to reflect lessons learnt inside a multistakeholder group. In this sense, the groups can become constrained by their organizational form.

These identified organizational beliefs and organizational forms for particular multistakeholder groups are closely inter-connected. Concern over asserting democratic principles is built in to the organizational belief that it is possible to identify all relevant stakeholders and incorporate them well into the organizational design of the multistakeholder project. Likewise, the organizational beliefs that multistakeholder groups can operate in a full disclosure mode and with an equitable internal decision-making system are reflective of the efforts of key participants to build a better governance process that they feel will resonate well with their aspirations for a new global democratic system. Similarly, organizational forms, like the one-big-table model and the governing council elected by independent chambers (for proper descriptions see below) are also efforts to construct a governance system that tilts intentionally in a democratic mode.

Nine beliefs and their governance consequences

The nine organizational beliefs involve the perception of the state of global affairs, the role of the new governance unit, the need for an inclusive structure, the connection between the sponsoring organization and its representative, the expectation that governance should be done by volunteers, that conflicts of interest can be internally managed, that decision-making is not autocratic, that the enterprise is robust, and that disclosure will be well managed. Organizational beliefs about the new governance unit are reinforced by the core notion that all "stakeholders" can be represented in each individual multistakeholder group. Consequently, the organizational belief that decision-making can be reasonably democratic is closely aligned with the belief that disclosure and management of conflicts can be achieved within a solid democratic framework.

Unsolved global problems

Multistakeholder governance arrangements are seen by participants as a structure that can produce a "solution" to the failure of multilateralism to address a specific global crisis or concern. A corollary of this belief is that, as the old order has not found a way to fix a global problem, a multistakeholder group and its participants should be granted a special form of legitimacy as they are taking up a challenge that has stumped governments. The GRI report presents this belief in a slightly different fashion. It argues that when nation-states fail to act, public actors should not be surprised if "plurilateral, often multistakeholder, coalitions of the willing and able" get active on a given international problem (WEF 2010: 30).

Structural and institutional characteristics 85

The *Global Governance 2025* report, jointly authored by the US National Intelligence Council and the EU Institute for Security Studies (ISS 2010: 33) summarizes the organizational consequences of this belief as follows:

> In some cases, innovative approaches stem from dissatisfaction with the relative inertia of traditional frameworks or with their perceived Western bias. Such approaches often involve "lighter" forms of cooperation than the highly legalized regimes inherited from the 20th century: consultation replaces regulation, codes of conduct prevail on binding norms, regional initiatives escape lengthy debates in multilateral forums, and national prerogatives trump international authorities in implementing and overseeing agreements.

The social definition of "unsolved problems" is at the heart of this organizational belief. Multistakeholder groups often state a particular unsolved problem in structural terms – for example, "preventing hunger in the world" – but operationalize it within their organization by selecting a far more limited issue area, such as providing capital to purchase seeds, fertilizers, and other small farm needs.

Two consequences of using this social definition of unsolved problems are relevant. First, given the composition of multistakeholder groups, it is unimaginable that a multistakeholder group is going to lead a global revolution – or even to call for one – to solve a structural failure of globalization. Almost by definition, key participants in a multistakeholder group have very great vested political and economic interests in the current structure of the global system, some of which contain inherent barriers to tackling issues such as global hunger and food insecurity. No multistakeholder group could directly challenge the vested interests of its key participants without these powerful institutional actors taking advantage of the voluntary nature of multistakeholderism and withdrawing or threatening to withdraw. The function of this organizational belief is to provide a multistakeholder group with a strong moral imperative for the joint undertaking which the participants understand will only address far more limited problems. The terms of reference of the multistakeholder group can only address carefully tailored, discrete unsolved problems within the current political-economic system.

The second consequence of this organizational belief is, for certain participants in a multistakeholder project and for the multistakeholder group's external relations, the convenience of being able to assert both goals at the same time. Part of the external audience and some of the participants may hear the high moral challenge as being at the heart of the multistakeholder project without noticing the clearly limited function the group sets for itself. Another part of the external audience and other participants may welcome the limited challenge as a worthy public policy goal

86 *Structural and institutional characteristics*

while they perceive that the solution to the limited challenge is a small step toward the more ambitions moral claim.

The governance consequences of this two-level understanding of "unsolved problems" is itself two-fold. First, it provides the multistakeholder group with a high moral claim that can help keep participants engaged in finding a pragmatic political compromise, even when the less demanding goal does not sufficiently bind the group. Second, the projection of a two-tiered definition of unsolved global problems dampens down other international efforts to address the broader structural deficit. Multistakeholderism's moral claims to address large-scale "unsolved problems" is closely aligned with its new governance concept.

"Stakeholders" as a meaningful governance category

Participants believe that an organization or individual who is designated a "stakeholder" appropriately joins "citizen" or "government" as the fundamental unit of legitimate political decision-making. A first corollary belief is that if one is a stakeholder, then one has a legitimate right to be a global decision-maker. A second is that both institutions – those who are part of the problem and those who are part of the solution – can have, in principle, equal status in governing as "stakeholders."

In multistakeholderism, the transition from persons, citizens, and nation-states as the fundamental units of governance has been extended to give quasi-legal status to "stakeholders." The power to declare an organization or individual a "stakeholder" is the power to elevate that category of actors to a global governance role while at the same time declaring that other categories of actors are marginal or illegitimate actors in global governance.

The organizational importance of this transformation is four-fold. Within a multistakeholder group, stakeholders perceive that, as they have the most clearly articulated and identified stake in an issue, they are the most legitimate actors to make governance rules for this issue area. They see themselves – and act as if – they, alongside other stakeholders, are the best suited to set the rules and practices for a given market. Under multistakeholderism, TNCs are joined by other actors, all of whom are seen by external observers as equal stakeholders, asserting that their expertise and business perspective can best govern a specific policy area. If a multistakeholder group does develop in a favorable direction for the key stakeholders, the more powerful actors can leave the group and effectively deprive others of their stakeholder governance status.

The second organizational consequence is that others, designated de facto "non-stakeholders," are presumed to benefit from choices that are made by stakeholder bodies. If these non-stakeholders do not share the belief that they are well served by stakeholder-centered decision-making, there is little opportunity for them to challenge the designation of their institution as a non-governing stakeholder.

The third consequence of shifting from the nation-states as the exclusive unit of international governance to stakeholder-based governance is the ambiguous status of the previous 400-year history of international obligations, liabilities, and responsibilities of the nation-state. The simple lack of clarity leaves stakeholders, as replacements for the nation-state, as key decision-makers without any legal or social consequences that may derive from their actions or non-actions in international governance.

Finally, the organizational consequence of the belief in stakeholders as the fundamental unit of global governance is that "citizens" and "people," all seven billion of them, are further disenfranchised from the process of global governance. As they are not designated as stakeholders, they have no institutional platform to express their views or to influence the outcome of a particular multistakeholder project. Simultaneously, and in tension with this idea, it is claimed that any given multistakeholder group can in fact be structurally inclusive.

The ability to identify all relevant stakeholders

Everyone who is affected by a problem can supposedly be represented inside a multistakeholder group. Underpinning this sentiment is the corollary belief that a greater diversity of actors around the table ensures a greater level of popular democracy. Both of these beliefs are presented as evidence that multistakeholderism is more democratic than multilateralism. As considered in Chapter 3, the foundation of and boundaries around any given stakeholder category are ambiguous. Consequently, whether the convener aggregates different constituencies into one super-category or disaggregates a category to smaller sub-categories, which can of course be further disaggregated, the resulting net effect is that claims of effective inclusion are an unobtainable goal.

Two examples will illustrate this organizational belief. For instance, the FAO's Committee on Food Security operationally defines "stakeholders" in food security as those with commercial involvement in food production, distribution, or processing, and those who are involved in agricultural development broadly defined. But it quite safe to say that food security rather involves everyone on the planet who has to eat.

Similarly, it is asserted that all stakeholders are engaged when an organization creates a diverse board to show that all major sectors of the public are involved, even when functionally the organization is not diverse. For example, the Global Compact has a lead body consisting of selected leaders from four constituencies – the business community, the trade union movement, NGOs, and the UN Secretariat. It is clear however that this does not reflect the membership of the Global Compact, nor its primary goals, as most active members of the Compact's lead body are TNCs. However, the four-part composition of the governing body is presented to the public to convey the view that the Global Compact is an all-inclusive organization.[1]

Table 4.1 Examples of assertions that all relevant stakeholders participate in a multistakeholder group

Name of stakeholder group	Scope of activity	Organizational assertions regarding all relevant stakeholders
Global Water Partnership	Improve water management	"Good water governance isn't going to happen unless there is an all-of-society involvement. That takes a credible, neutral, experienced, multistakeholder network […] only when a broad range of stakeholders work together will we change water management for the better."
World Ocean Council	Corporate ocean sustainability	"The breadth of our partnerships, including intergovernmental bodies, governments, business associations and foundations, NGOs and others enables us to effectively develop and advance the 'Corporate Ocean Responsibility' agenda of the Ocean Business Community."
ICANN	Internet governance	"ICANN is committed to its multistakeholder model of governance and believes that global inclusivity, transparency and accountability are critical to being trusted by its stakeholders worldwide to fulfill its Mission."

Sources: Global Water Partnership 2017; World Ocean Council n.d.; ICANN 2014.

Additional examples of the organizational belief that all relevant stakeholders can be meaningfully involved with a multistakeholder group are presented in Table 4.1.

The hardest community to identify may well be those peoples and communities that might be most adversely affected by the actions of a given multistakeholder group. Environmental impact statements were designed to identify downstream secondary or tertiary consequences of a public policy or a construction project. In the governance arena, if a multistakeholder group takes an action which has a secondary or tertiary impact on gender equality, it is very difficult – if not impossible – for the founders of a multistakeholder group to assert honestly that everyone who is impacted is brought on board. As the test standards for reliably determining downstream impacts have not yet been developed for multistakeholderism, it is very difficult to be confident that all relevant stakeholders are invited into the process.

Widely expressed claims that "all relevant stakeholders are represented" foster a false sense that democratic principles are built into multistakeholder governance. Those asserting that all relevant stakeholders are involved are in effect distracting attention from the exclusivity of a multistakeholder group. The composition of almost all multistakeholder groups is the result of a management-based selection process. An organizational belief that it is possible to have an inclusive process is an illusionary governance goal for multistakeholderism. The belief that all relevant stakeholders are represented also involves an unclear relationship between an organizational stakeholder and their representative in a multistakeholder group.

A participant brings the support of their organization or sector

A good number of multistakeholder groups believe that having an individual from a TNC, international CSO, or a government participate in the leadership of their organization means that that the TNC, CSO, or government itself is on board. This particular organizational belief is at the heart of the asserted representativeness of organizational members of a multistakeholder group.

As each of these stakeholder categories are very large institutions, the participation of a representative from these bodies may only mean that a particular office or department has chosen to work with that multistakeholder group. The participation of any individual does not itself mean that the sponsoring organization as a whole is committed politically or economically to that multistakeholder group. The individual involved may only have been granted permission to work with a given multistakeholder group or provided leave to participate in their personal, professional capacity. This ambiguity between the commitment of the institution as a whole and the participation by a representative of a specific office or agency can affect a number of different roles inside and outside the multistakeholder group. The multistakeholder group may well appreciate being able to assert publicly that x government or y TNC is part of the multistakeholder group in order to garner greater political and/or economic recognition. Internally, the other participants may believe that the institutional capacities and financial resources of the parent organization may be available to meet the goals of the multistakeholder group.

A corollary to this organizational belief is that having a TNC, an international CSO, or a government involved in a multistakeholder group implies that in some way TNCs, civil society, and governments in general are on board. This organizational belief can have some significant public consequences. It may appear to members of the public that a particular economic sector, a particular social community, or a group of governments are on board with this initiative and dissuade them from taking other political-economic or public policy actions of their own, in the expectation that the problem is being handled by the key governance groups writ large; not just that the particular office or particular organization is participating in the multistakeholder group.

Another, related, corollary to this organizational belief is that individuals in some multistakeholder groups take part only in their personal professional capacity and not as representatives of their government, CSO, or TNC. And a variant of this organizational belief also applies to the status of religious leaders and academics participating in a multistakeholder group. Yet, when the multistakeholder group publishes the names of these individual leaders, their names are routinely supplemented with their current organizational affiliation. If it is indeed the case that these individuals are only participating in their personal, professional capacity, then it is unnecessary to include as the key element of their professional biography the name of their current employer.

The level of commitment by the organizational sponsor can be significantly affected by the belief that membership is understood to be a volunteer activity.

Volunteerism as a necessary condition

Advocates of multistakeholderism believe that all multistakeholder undertakings need to be based on voluntary participation. The corollary here is that, without a voluntary system, some of the potential major non-state actors would opt not to participate in a multistakeholder project. Table 4.2 has examples of calls for volunteer participation in multistakeholder groups.

The belief in the need for volunteerism in governance resolves a number of complicated issues. It means that key actors can join or abstain, as and when it best suits them. Find the right combination of government offices, the most interested global corporations, and the best informed civil society experts and let them find the right solution. Others from international, regional, and local communities, businesses, or governments can join the volunteer team over time.

The WEF's contribution is to assert that volunteering on a global level leads to more effective decision-making than the decision-making of UN system bodies. Identified problems can be addressed more quickly without, in their view, recalcitrant government officials, old-fashioned narrow-minded business executives, and divergent views from civil society. The WEF also argues that the outcome of the process will have greater legitimacy, as the key TNCs and other interested constituencies are seen as working together. In short, this organizational belief means that those who want to participate can do so, and those who do not want to participate can stay out of the process. The fact that the non-participants stay on the sidelines is not seen as a particular hindrance; at least, it is less a market hindrance than the articulation of soft law intergovernmental standards would be.

Volunteerism can proffer quick fixes. Twenty organizations can gather, including some which are either the cause or partial cause of a problem, and some of which have the economic, social, or military clout to fix a problem. For those twenty and hopefully some others positively influenced

Table 4.2 Examples of calls for volunteer participation by multistakeholder groups

Organization	Scope of activity	Calls for volunteer participation
Bali Principles for multistakeholder partnerships	Agenda 21 and Millennium Development Goals	"Partnerships should be voluntary and self-organizing."
A Guide for National ICT Policy Animators	ICT policy advocacy	"These partnerships are voluntary, with participation driven by perceived benefits [the participants] may see emerging from the process."
General Assembly Resolution on Partnerships for Development		Defines [global partnerships] as "voluntary and collaborative relationships between various parties, both public and non-public, in which all participants agree to work together to achieve a common purpose or undertake a specific task and, as mutually agreed, to share risks and responsibilities, resources and benefits."
Global Partnership for Effective Development Co-operation	Achievement of Sustainable Development Goals	Tracks progress in the implementation of these principles (SDGs) through its voluntary and country-led monitoring process.
Alliance for Responsible Mining	Socially and environmentally sustainable sector	"People who serve on ARM's Board of Directors do so voluntarily and without monetary remuneration."

Sources in order cited: Pattberg 2012; Adam et al. 2007: 5; UN 2008; Global Partnership for Effective Development Co-operation 2017; Alliance for Responsible Mining n.d.

by the leadership of the twenty, something constructive might happen. But even five times this number of organizations does not make a global change; it only shifts the behavior for the few that are engaged. When one or two TNC executives cycle out, when one or two governments shift their attention, when the international media reduces its attention to an issue, or when one or two other volunteers focus on the next matter, there is no longer an institutional base to move forward, particularly as there are also another 100 TNCs, another twenty governments, and another set of non-state actors which are committed to keeping things as they were before the initial twenty volunteers started their multistakeholder meetings. Changing the harmful behavior of a group of international actors is very important, but it does not equate to effective or meaningful global governance. And it could open wider opportunities for non-participants – whose activities include the undesirable practices – to expand their activities in a socially or environmentally harmful direction.

If a commercial partner walks away from a voluntary PPP, it can leave the remaining state bodies, international organizations, or the CSO groups with the political liabilities for a perceived failure. If a significant CSO withdraws, it can change the balance of power within a PPP, but it does not necessarily mean the PPP will collapse or immediately lose legitimacy with local authorities or the wider community. In a similar manner to project-based PPPs, TNCs can join a multistakeholder governance process if and when it looks lucrative or provides other benefits to the firm.

In both situations, there tends to be a quiet recruitment of participants into a multistakeholder process or, as WEF sometimes calls them, "coalitions of the willing and able." A civil society group may join a multistakeholder process and then subsequently decide that their financially constrained organization has other priorities. A government body may choose to participate in starting a multistakeholder process to gain public visibility, but does not have the energy or resources to engage effectively over the long term. As all participants are voluntary actors, any of them can withdraw whenever they wish.

An organizational belief in the necessity of voluntary engagement presumes that the spirit of cooperation prevails in international relations, not that the underlying reality of both multilateralism and multistakeholderism is a conflict-based world. In the multilateral world, the central conflicts are seen as those between nation-states. In a multistakeholder world, the degree of conflict does not necessarily decline and nor does the degree of cooperation increase. The conflicts between governments remain and the additional actors add their own intra-stakeholder and inter-stakeholder conflicts as background to the decisions of the multistakeholder group. As a result, there are more conflicts to be managed in multistakeholderism than in multilateralism.

Allied to the organizational belief in volunteerism is the idea that all the participants have reasonably equal amounts of time, energy, and capital to contribute to the multistakeholder group. As with other resources, there is unequal access to "volunteer time." Some participants are on full organizational salaries, some are unpaid, and some have to raise funds to support their involvement. As some participants can attend meetings regularly and others only sporadically, the unequal access to volunteer time is also a challenge for the democratic internal decision-making process. Compensating for the imbalance in available volunteer time is only one element that needs to be addressed to have a democratic internal governance system.

Equitable decision-making

Many multistakeholder groups operate with the belief that internal decision-making can be made reasonably equitable, even with inherent asymmetries of power. Similarly, there is a belief that the lack of a commonly accepted set of rules for multistakeholder governance is not an impediment to good internal governance. A second corresponding belief is that all stakeholders share a willingness to have an equitable decision-making structure.

Few multistakeholder groups start out with a written rule book laying out the appropriate ways to make legitimate decisions, reconcile opposing views, or protect minority views. An organizational consequence of this belief is that internal governance tends to be a largely ad hoc system, developed either on the fly or in response to a particular internal power struggle within a given multistakeholder group.[2] In the field of environmental and social multistakeholder standard-setting, ISEAL, the major trade association of these groups, has an extensive set of guidance manuals for assisting its members with their standard-setting, certifying, and verifying missions, but it does not have a guidance document on how to operate democratically within multistakeholder standard-setting organizations.

By contrast, some large established multistakeholder groups, like ISO and ICANN, have internal rule books that cover a wide range of governance decision-making matters and are hundreds of pages long. It is worth noting that these organizational rule books have chosen different ways to institutionalize a belief in equitable decision-making. As with multilateralism, the definition of "consensus decision-making" has multiple meanings. The comprehensiveness and the uniqueness of these rule books has an institutional downside. New participants and non-participants cannot easily understand how the organizational belief in equitable decision-making works in particular situations and how the rules might mediate pre-existing external conflicts. Some core elements of a basic rule book for multistakeholder internal governance are provided in Chapter 5.

Managing conflicts of interest

The belief here is that conflicts within stakeholder categories, conflicts between stakeholder categories, and commercial conflicts of interest can be overcome by finding a shared view about the seriousness of an unsolved global issue. The corollary is that participants in multistakeholder groups believe that, if there is a sufficiently high degree of shared concerns and goals, intra-stakeholder conflicts, inter-stakeholder conflicts, and business conflicts of interest can be managed so as not to hinder the effective functioning of the multistakeholder group. One organizational consequence of this belief is that advocates for multistakeholderism emphasize that participants should seek to identify areas of mutual self-interest in order to manage intra-stakeholder and inter-stakeholder conflicts.

However, in a globalized economy, TNCs fight for market share, for better returns on investment, for quality workers, for the recruitment of executives, and for access to natural resources. CSOs fight with other

CSOs for membership, access to funding, the appropriateness of their ideological approaches, and their strategic and tactical choices for effecting change. Government participants have intra-departmental conflicts, opposition to governments in other geopolitical groups, and sometimes conflicts with other branches of their own government. Other categories of stakeholders from religious leaders to academics have their own level of intra-sectorial conflicts.

Each of these categories of stakeholders has structural conflicts with other categories of stakeholders. If a multistakeholder group is to function successfully or to endure over time, the organizational challenge is to elevate attention to the shared goals while minimizing institutional conflicts. A consequence of the latter step is that the suppression of real-world conflicts tends to restrict the development of ideas to address a problem out of a concern that one or more participants is likely to be hostile to the idea.

As discussed in Chapter 1, the definition of "conflict of interest" may need special attention in a multistakeholder world. The organizational belief that this can be managed depends to a large degree on whether there is an organizational platform for participants and non-participants to assert that a conflict of interest may exist, or for a commercial actor to recuse themselves from a particular multistakeholder action because of the existence or appearance of existence of such a conflict of interest. The organizational challenge here is to balance expectations that the group can manage internal and external conflicts with the reality that there are often real conflicts of interest that should exclude the participation of some members of a multistakeholder group from some elements of the decision-making.

The more challenging definitional issue is how to manage conflicts of interest that may have an ideological element that restricts a multistakeholder group from moving in a pragmatic direction. If a trade association member or a government member of a multistakeholder group is only able to accept market-based solutions to a given global problem, there will be on-going tensions between the organizational belief that conflicts can be managed and the likelihood of discovering innovative solutions.

Clearly, some institutions that are seen as stakeholders are part of the problem, or have a high degree of self-interest in ensuring that any proposed policy or solution does not run counter to their perceived self-interests. Some major stakeholder may well seek to join a multistakeholder group primarily to further their business model and may see broader social-political goals as of minor importance to their firm. Other stakeholders may use a multistakeholder group's platform to advance their organizational agenda, potentially disregarding specific social-environmental goals that the group intends to address. In this sense, the organizational belief that stakeholder category conflicts and conflicts of interest can be effectively ignored may set a multistakeholder group up for an on-going governance challenge. Such internal tensions do not always contribute to a productive work environment or to one that can necessarily be effective or efficient.

Enhanced efficiency and effectiveness

Another organizational belief is that decisions can be made faster and projects implemented more effectively than could be done by the UN system or governments. A complementary belief is that corporate management experience can be effectively transferred to the public arena.

Judging the relative effectiveness and efficiency of decision-making and of project implementation in global governance requires one of two functional options: a baseline for comparison or the ability to compare the situation to the counter-factual or a no-action scenario. In the former case, missing data for a baseline and the impossibility to measure with explicit variables effectively precludes a documented conclusion. In the latter case, the bar can be set so low as to be relatively meaningless or the bar can be set so high that it prevents a meaningful analytic assessment. As with other real organizational beliefs, the beliefs themselves have a power beyond their evidential basis.

The claim that corporate management experience can be transferred to the global public arena in a meaningful manner is undocumented. The operational belief is that by bringing TNCs management skills on board, the effectiveness of the undertaking will be well secured. It is not clear, however, if corporate effectiveness measures are fundamentally identical or can be aligned harmoniously with effective global governance measures. In the business world, effectiveness is recognized by increases in sales, decreases in production costs per unit of sales, or through increases in uses or markets for technologies and services or similar profit-maximizing outcomes. In the public governance world, corporate executives may well use their experiences to reduce operating costs but not any of the other corporate-recognized measures of effectiveness.

The disconnect between corporate management measures of effectiveness and efficiency and global governance measurement of these fundamental criteria extends to the knowledge base and the performance standards of good corporate executives. As presented in the GRI, corporate management successes are based on a sound knowledge of a given market segment (WEF 2010: 117). Market success comes from narrowing the knowledge base of corporate executives to the specific features that may influence their particular market. This narrowing is so necessary for corporate management success that the WEF recommends future global corporate executives receive support and training from leaders of civil society about the wider implications of global governance. Phrased in a different fashion, one of the successes for corporate managers is to externalize costs related to their product-process markets. For a successful role in global governance management, the corporate management approach now needs to consider how to deliver the services that their business practices have been externalizing.

Further, one cannot operate a global governance system with a mindset that, if a specific products-process does not meet operational expectations, one simply sells the firm or drops out of the market. If a PPP has taken on the responsibility to meet a public need, the PPP cannot simply "sell the need" to another consortium. All meaningful corporate measures of effectiveness and efficiency also presume a stable institutional base, not one where there could be potential shifts in institutional actors and underlying bureaucratic structures. Global governance is an on-going process that cannot simply be shut down if management goals are not met.

Dingwerth and Pattberg (2009: 718–19) take a different approach to assessing the organizational belief in the relative efficiency and effectiveness in multistakeholderism:

> Efficiency-based approaches have highlighted the possibility of realizing mutually beneficial agreements among cooperating partners and of reducing transaction costs. Seen in this way, the Forest Stewardship Council, for instance, is an institution in which NGOs grant legitimacy in exchange for influence on the behaviour of wood retailers. For the latter, the equation is the reverse – they give others a say in determining their corporate behaviour and receive an increase in social acceptance and reputation. For both sides, cost–benefit calculations are positive. Provided that neither of the two sides has a better alternative, this explains why they cooperate. In this view, a particular organizational design may be seen either as a compromise between NGOs' desire for influence and corporations' desire not to be influenced too much – in other words, as the price to be paid for the level of legitimacy they seek – or simply as the most efficient means to fulfil the organization's functions, including to raise awareness, increase social acceptance and improve the substantive quality of decisions.

The issue of effectiveness is addressed in a different manner by The Global Challenges Foundation. It notes that the effective governance of new technologies may well require TNC involvement, including even those TNCs that hold a patent or license for a given technology, because rules will not be able to be drafted without their expertise. The argument is premised in part on the first organizational belief above (the recognition that governments and the UN system are not going to act) so that some rule-making involving TNCs may be the only effective option on the table:

> For a long time, the private sector has been part of the problem. Involving private sector entities in decision-making on global governance issues may therefore be necessary to stop further damage and

develop new standards for voluntary action, as well as new regulations. This was one of the main reasons why the Convention on Biological Diversity engaged actively with the private sector.... It is ... hard to imagine the public sector and the third sector making progress on governance architectures, particularly those involving new technologies, without a substantial role for the private sector.

(Joshi 2016)

Getting anywhere from one to a dozen members of a multistakeholder group to change is a major accomplishment. The tendency to extrapolate from a small sample the relative effectiveness and efficiency of a multistakeholder project to the multistakeholder world is always tempting but without analytic merit. The organizational belief in the greater power of multistakeholderism as an effective and efficient governance instrument often rests on claims of success for specific multistakeholder projects. It has not been – and probably cannot be – used to constrain the negative behavior of powerful actors which choose not to join a multistakeholder group or to follow their voluntary lead. One reason to self-appraise one's own multistakeholder group is to be able to honestly share the results with the wider community.

On transparency

The ninth organizational belief is a belief that high levels of disclosure, public accounting, and transparency will permit the public to engage meaningfully with a multistakeholder group. Here the corollary belief is that openness or the willingness to be open will enhance the legitimacy of a given multistakeholder group.

It is not clear if the expectation for disclosure, public accounting, and transparency applies exclusively to the multistakeholder group itself or to the multistakeholder group and to each member of its governing body. The ambiguity is such that each participant of the governing body may properly be expected to be transparent about what it contributes financially, intellectually, and politically while the multistakeholder group may be expected to be transparent about what it does with these resources, how it plans to address an unsolved global matter, and how it appraises its accomplishment. Because of the diverse structures of multistakeholder groups, it is often hard to tell who to congratulate or who to blame if the "problem" does not go away.

Without a clear sense of accountability, a significant number of citizens lose a sense of public participation in governance and become disillusioned with the legitimacy of government. Similarly, at the global level opt-in/opt-out governance discourages long-term institutional engagement, leaving active participation to those who hold a strong organizational base that can benefit from their volunteer engagement – i.e., international firms and the nation-state. Without a sense of accountability toward the broader community, the legitimacy of globalization will remain unsettled.

The belief is often greater than the practice, as the levels of provision of information outside the multistakeholder group is quite uneven. In a review of over 100 websites on multistakeholder governance, there was none with a formal line-by-line budget, none with the disclosure of specific income from major individual donors or income from specific product or process activities, and few including salaries and benefits of senior staff. All of these reporting standards are now expected in government and corporate reports. None of the websites for organizations that cited UN soft law statements or their commitment to the implementation of the SDGs provided a copy of any report to an intergovernmental body. At a more general level, the General Assembly after eight resolutions "Towards Global Partnerships" dating back to 2001 is still just stressing the need for the UN system to develop a common and systemic approach to "transparency, coherence, impact, accountability, and due diligence" (UN 2015a).

Gasser et al. (2015: 21) came to a similar assessment, writing:

> In the same way that the tools of inclusiveness are often deployed in instrumental ways to achieve strategic objectives, transparency is also an instrumental tool within [our] case studies. The case studies show that often the level of transparency that a governance group uses can be moderated to the specific needs and circumstances that the group faces over its lifecycle.

Another inconsistency in transparency practice applies to the issue of conflicts of interest. In none of the websites reviewed was there a clear policy statement about how conflicts of commercial interests were to be identified or addressed. There was also no indication whether specific stakeholders received waivers from the organizational conflict of interest rules or there were voluntary recusals from decision-making by individual stakeholders.

These nine organizational beliefs are central to the operations of almost all of the multistakeholder groups examined. To the non-participant, they are often presented to demonstrate that a multistakeholder approach is a sounder route forward, or that a multistakeholder approach is a more democratic arrangement than multilateralism. For the participants, these beliefs tend to guide the day-to-day operation of multistakeholder planning, even though the organizational belief itself has not been tested or validated. They also tend to influence the organizational form of each individual multistakeholder group; these forms and their governance consequences are considered below.

Structural and institutional characteristics of multistakeholder governance

As multistakeholderism is a relatively new global governance phenomenon, its structural and institutional characteristics are quite fluid. This high degree of organizational experimentation ranges from parallel intergovernmental and non-state oversight of UN system bodies to various arrangements of multi-chamber bodies. In this period of growth and transition, a number of scholars have tried to create typologies of multistakeholder institutional arrangements.[3] This section takes a different approach. It provides introductory observations on four different organizational forms of self-standing multistakeholder projects; two forms of multistakeholder relationships involving the UN system; and one proposed structure involving the political management of zones of conflict.

The self-standing multistakeholder models include a one-big-table model, a multi-chamber system that elects a governing body, a multi-chamber system that advises a governing body, and a system of weighted stakeholder voting. The UN system structure includes a multistakeholder group as an adjunct of an international secretariat and a multistakeholder body meeting in parallel with multilateral governing bodies. These are not exclusive forms; some multistakeholder groups are a hybrid of different forms. All these organizational forms present different opportunities and challenges for democratic governance. This is not surprising, as the choice of form involves not only concerns about the externally accepted legitimacy of the process but also the beliefs of the convener and other founding members about how to create an organizational form that is in their thinking effective and efficient.

The one-big-table model

In the one-big-table model, there are a variety of chairs around the table assigned to designated organizations and/or individuals who, a convener appraises, are the best participants in a given process. In this model participants are given the opportunity to offer knowledge on an issue to all other participants and to learn without intermediation the perspectives and self-interests of all the other parties. The core strength of the one-big-table model is that it explicitly creates a physical space to build a community of shared constituencies, rather than segmenting potentially conflicting groups into different silos and then structurally devising methods to reconcile their diverse positions. In this sense, it functions in a similar fashion to a national parliament. Unlike national parliaments, however, the size of a multistakeholder one-big-table group is generally fewer than thirty chairs. Similar to national parliaments, however, the one-big-table model may create workgroups that address specific issues which report back to the overall membership. This model is a more likely format for multistakeholder groups endeavoring to create a global policy regime and for project-oriented multistakeholder groups rather than for multistakeholder standard-setting bodies.

Examples of this model include the Roundtable on Sustainable Soy with three major stakeholder categories and a maximum of five representatives each constituting the Executive Board; the Better Cotton Initiative whose Council has three seats for each of the four membership categories; the Global Reporting Initiative with four categories of stakeholders on its sixteen-member Board of Directors; and the World Economic Forum's Global Future Councils with twenty to twenty-five individuals selected to participate in each Council.

From a governance perspective, the one-big-table model has a number of matters that deserve reflection, including the presumed equality of seats around the table and the method of decision-making used. One consequence of the organizational belief in the importance of volunteerism is that any given chair around the table may or may not be filled at a given meeting depending on whether the individual participant has the time and other resources to attend. In this manner, those with an established organizational base and the financial resources to attend meetings can have a disproportionate impact on the outcome of the group, even though all participants have formal seats at the table.

How a one-big-table model makes formal decisions depends heavily on the role of the chair and the formal mechanisms adopted for "voting." "Voting" appears in quotation marks as a good number of one-big-table multistakeholder groups assert they function on consensus, on unanimity, or on non-objection basis. The rules – either formally adopted or informally understood – about how to challenge the claimed outcome of a multistakeholder meeting are then crucial.

These two elements – the presumed equivalence of participants in a multistakeholder group and the process for establishing organizational decisions – apply in large part as well to decision-making bodies with weighted categories and other forms of organizational multistakeholder groups.

A decision-making body explicitly weighted by stakeholder categories

Weighted decision-making involves establishing a governing system where certain categories of stakeholders are guaranteed more seats at the table than other categories. In many cases, the publicly available information about a particular multistakeholder group does not explain the rationale for the structural imbalance in the governing body. In some cases, it is possible to see why one stakeholder category is given extra designee seats or a higher fixed percentage of designees than others. These explanations include (1) participants may insist on a positive weighted balance for their stakeholder group as a condition for participating if they feel they are going to be routinely outvoted; (2) funders expect that they will be more comfortable as future sources of underwriting if they have a secured seat in a particular group; and (3) participants which have a dominant market position or a long-standing political role in a policy area may not join unless they believe that they will be able to continue to exercise their previous influence.

As an example, the weighted decision-making model is used by IUCN, the Roundtable on Sustainable Palm Oil, Fair Flowers Fair Plants, the Alliance for Responsible Mining, the International Organic Accreditation Service, and the Stop TB Partnership. The International Union for Conservation of Nature (IUCN) has a weighted voting system in which governments can have three votes; international NGOs have two votes; and national NGOs have one vote. The Roundtable on Sustainable Palm Oil has seven major stakeholder categories (oil palm growers, palm oil processors, consumer goods manufacturers, retailers, banks/investors, environmental NGOs, and social/development NGOs). Each category elects two members to the Board of Governors, except the oil palm growers group, which elects four members. Other weighted decision-making multistakeholder groups include the International Organic Accreditation Service, whose Board of Directors is formed by three individuals representing the developing world, three beneficiaries, two operators, and one individual representing the conformity assessments sector. The Board of Directors of the Stop TB Partnership has three representatives of financial donors, one representative of foundations, two seats for technical agencies, four seats for multilaterals, one representative of a developing country NGO, one representative of a developed country NGO, one representative of the private sector, two representatives of tuberculosis-affected communities, two representatives of their working groups, six from tuberculosis-affected countries, and two open seats.

From a democratic governance perspective, a weighted voting system is always problematic. In multilateralism, the weighted voting system in the IMF and World Bank and the special version of the weighted voting system in the Security Council have been areas of major tension for governments and others engaged with these bodies. Replicating explicit weighted voting in favor of more powerful members in a multistakeholder group offers no political or social advance in global governance over existing weighted voting systems in multilateralism. It might be possible to have a weighted voting system that promotes the under-represented geographic groups, stakeholders with limited effective voice in contemporary governance, or those most likely to be adversely affected. Determining the proper weights for this arrangement would clearly not be an easy task for a democratic system.

The informality of rules governing multistakeholderism can create a process of indirect weighted voting systems that can be as risky for democratic decision-making in global governance as explicitly weighted voting systems. Rather than formally declaring that X stakeholder gets a higher percentage of votes, a convener can sub-divide stakeholder group X into three or four sub-stakeholder categories where each of these sub-categories gets a seat at the table. The net effect on the democratic legitimacy may be the same, except that the latter approach is made to appear more equitable. For example, the rules for the twenty-two member governing body of the Global Compact state that the board members agree to strive for consensus, but, "in the event that complete consensus is not possible, substantial consensus of 2/3 majority will suffice" (Global Compact 2013). The net effect is that the six non-business members of the board cannot prevail on any issue without getting support from ten business leaders. On the other hand, the business members can make policy decisions without any support from the non-corporate members.

A governing council elected from stakeholder chambers

A governing council elected by multiple stakeholder chambers allows for competing interests and contrasting views of specific stakeholder groups to be openly recognized by giving each community a separate institutional base. In this manner, each key stakeholder community can work independently and collectively to address a common global issue. The premise is that the organizations in each chamber can more easily overcome differences in perspective by working only with their presumed similar bodies and that, with a resolution of intra-sectorial views, there will be a more secure platform for a healthy inter-chamber debate in the decision-making process. In some cases, the central governing body also has members that are independent from the competing constituencies.

This structure is used, for example, by the Extractive Industry Transparency Initiative, the Global Coffee Platform, and ICANN. For the Extractive Industries Transparency Initiative (EITI) globally and nationally, each category elects three representatives to the Board with an additional observer seat provided for the government (Vallejo and Hauselmann 2004). A second example is the Global Coffee Platform where their four categories – producers, trade, industry, and civil society – are all equally "represented in every governance organ and have equal decision-making powers" (Global Coffee Platform n.d.). ICANN's Board of Directors is composed of sixteen members nominated by the Supporting Organizations, the Nominating Committee and the At-Large Community (ICANN 2012).

As with weighted voting multistakeholder groups, a good deal rests on how the multistakeholder group operatizes the ambiguities in the boundaries of stakeholder categories. In the case of the Global Coffee Platform, the number of chambers could be reduced by grouping all the commercial entities together (producers, trade, and industry), or expanding them, as is the case with the Roundtable on Sustainable Palm Oil which now comprises seven commercial categories. Likewise, the civil society chamber could be sub-divided into civil society organizations, scientific bodies, and the general public. The net effort to enhance democracy within a governing system which elects the governing council from the individual chambers is plagued by an arbitrariness in the very definition of chambers.

A governing council advised by stakeholder chambers

By creating the governing council and two or more largely independent chambers of stakeholders, a multistakeholder organization can have the advantages of a hierarchical organization for operational decision-making while establishing a political space for key constituency groups to resolve intra-sector approaches and then provide their consensus recommendations to a leadership council. A multi-chamber advisory model means that the governing body has the challenge to reconcile competing or antagonistic positions between constituencies, but they also gain the flexibility to find a middle position between the separate advisory chambers. In a sense, this is a balancing act, one-part traditional vertical control and one-part horizontal consideration of an issue. With an advisory structure, the chambers can debate key issues openly, without the responsibility of turning these debates necessarily into detailed decisions applicable to all related parties. For this advisory structure to be effective, the advisory chambers need a set of rules to balance intra-constituency power differentials, rules similar to those in the UN system to provide smaller and politically weaker governments equity in dealing with more powerful states. As partly a traditional organization, an independent governing council is similar to the board of a non-profit organization or a corporation. It has the full legal authority to act, can meet legal requirements for organizational liability and reporting, and can have a clear method to maintain itself over time. The rules of procedure and the informal practices between the governing council and the advisory chambers vary widely.

The Marine Stewardship Council is a good example of the diversity of internal structures for governing councils advised by multiple chambers. The co-convening organizations, Unilever and WWF, established a Board of Trustees/Directors as the lead body for the Marine Stewardship Council and an advisory Stakeholder Council which consisted of two separate chambers. One chamber was designed to reflect commercial interests and the other to reflect the public interest. The commercial chamber is made up of enterprises that catch, process, supply, retail, provide food services, and other relevant fish-related food industries. The public interest chamber is composed of academics, scientists, management, the marine conservation community, and other civil society organizations. Half of the nominations for membership of the advisory Stakeholder Council come from the Board of Trustees/Directors and the other half from the chambers. The co-chairs of the Stakeholder Council are members of the Board of Trustees.

104 *Structural and institutional characteristics*

This model of governing council with advisory sub-bodies was also used by the twelve-member Commission on Dams (WCD) which established a sixty-eight-member WCD Forum. The Commission's chair described the relationship between the Commission and its Forum as one where the Forum "had no formal role in the mandate of the WCD. Instead, it constituted a reference body, a corps of advisors, and a bouncing board for the Commission" (Asmal 2001: 1415). Another example of this model is the SA 8000 Board of Directors, the governing body of Social Accountability International, which is supported by an Advisory Board of up to twenty-five people, equally balanced between their two stakeholder categories – business and non-business members. The non-business category includes NGOs, trade unions, socially responsible investors, and governments; the business category includes media, automotive, fashion and steel companies.

From a governance perspective, there are two crucial consequences – one internal and one external – from the advisory chamber governance model. Internally, the separate chambers are largely kept apart from each other and from the central governing body. This split between the chambers means that the outcome is not necessarily a commonly accepted compromise position between all the internal actors. The governing body can make the crucial decisions, providing it can maintain credibility with its chamber advisors. This is somewhat analogous to a government agency collecting input from key constituencies and then making an administrative decision. However, the wider community may come to believe that the outcome from this type of multistakeholder group is in fact a consensus position between all the applicable constituencies. This inconsistency between the internal advisory function to the decision-making bodies and the external view that this is a form of multistakeholder governance is troubling.

International secretariat-led multistakeholder groups

Under multistakeholderism, there has been an accelerating speed of change toward quasi-independent secretariats at each UN system body. International secretariat involvement in multistakeholder governance involves both UN system staff participating in externally organized multistakeholder groups and UN system staff creating multistakeholder groups as adjunct organizations of the secretariat. As noted in Chapter 3, UN system staff participating in externally organized multistakeholder groups have little or no policy supervision at the intergovernmental level. These staff may well take time away from their formally assigned responsibilities to participate in externally organized multistakeholder groups.

The most well-known multistakeholder groups convened by an international secretariat are the Global Compact, Every Woman Every Child,[4] and Sustainable Energy for All (SE4All).[5] These three initiatives were created under the authority of the UN Secretary-General's office without any formal authorization from an intergovernmental body and without pre-approval of work plans or policy directions. Subsequently, to minimize efforts by the General Assembly's committees to have more oversight, the latter two organizations were moved out of the UN Secretary-General's office to be under the authority of the Executive Director of UNESCO in Paris and a new "non-profit, independent Quasi-International Organization" headquartered in Vienna, respectively.

The SE4All partnership reflects the changed role of the international secretariat. The project diverges from intergovernmental practice in three ways. On the policy side, the multistakeholder bodies adjunct to the secretariat consider that they can modify the General Assembly's policy positions to accommodate the concerns of potential members of a UN system–private sector partnership. For example, the SE4All revised the SDG commitment on energy. The approved SDG 7, which is summarized on the SDG logo as "Affordable and Clean Energy," formally reads, "By 2030, ensure universal access to affordable, reliable and modern energy services" (SDG goal 7.1, UN 2015b). The related SE4All goal is "Ensuring universal access to modern energy services," deleting the commitment to affordability and reliability.

A second feature of UN system-hosted multistakeholder groups is that this arrangement circumvents intergovernmental approval of individual TNCs and other participants in UN partnerships. Under the Partnership Office, firms can work under the UN without any formal registration review, except a generic statement of support for the SDGs and the payment of membership fees in selected situations. This means that the structure allows the heads of UN organizations to accept TNCs as legitimate UN partners without having to receive or accept policy guidance from the intergovernmental membership. In the case of SE4All, this means that coal and oil companies can participate as full members, even if their fundamental activity and public positions are out of line with the Paris climate agreement.

The third feature of quasi-autonomous international secretariat system multistakeholder groups is that TNCs and other actors can assert that they are in partnership with the UN system, even if their level of engagement is limited to one UN system-related activity. Until the 1990s, the UN Legal Counsel's Office reviewed and carefully approved or disapproved all formal public assertions involving the UN's name by commercial organizations. As part of the transition to multistakeholderism, the UN now allows TNCs to gain public relations advantage from even a low level of commitment. TNCs are allowed to use their UN identification when and where it might help them with their marketing, which is seen by some TNCs as relevant to their public relations in selected markets.

Unlike the business world, partnerships between the UN system and the commercial world do not need a formal written document that makes commitments about the allocation of inputs, the distribution of risks, and the terms for terminating the arrangement. Without such a publicly accessible document, the asymmetric balance of power within a partnership involving UN system staff is likely to favor the corporate side at the expense of civil society and the UN. And without a clear formal document, intergovernmental review or even ex-post reviews have little basis for holding the UN system secretariat or its organizational partners accountable.

Multistakeholder bodies parallel to intergovernmental bodies

GRI recommends that, when a UN system governing body is meeting, there should be a separate parallel governing meeting with key non-state actors. As good case studies, GRI identified two UN specialized agencies: WHO and UNESCO.

> "A set of **proposals to strengthen global health governance,** including an annual multi-actor Global Health Summit adjacent to the World Health Organization's intergovernmental World Health Assembly."
> (WEF 2010: 14; bold in the original)

> "... there is a notable lack of high-level political commitment, a comparatively weak and poorly resourced set of international institutions and an insufficient emphasis on practical, results-oriented alliances, including those involving the business community. In response, the [GRI Council] has proposed a multi-stakeholder review of the structure and capacity of the [UNESCO] Education for All architecture."
> (WEF 2010: 32)

The premise behind parallel sessions for multilateral bodies and multistakeholder bodies is to bridge a significant governance gap. When intergovernmental bodies articulate new soft law positions, all too often these new soft law standards can be just words on paper. Part of the reason for this governance failure is the non-mandatory nature of these resolutions and the autonomy of the globalization process from the UN system. TNCs get to decide if and when they will act in accordance with the intergovernmental soft law decisions, as there is no risk for them from noncompliance. In this sense the autonomy means that TNCs can have a de facto final vote on the implementation of any new UN-sponsored soft law. Similarly, when the UN system makes programmatic decisions that involve other international actors, these actors get to decide if and when they will respond to the call. In all too many cases, the program is under-implemented when other international actors choose not to follow up. GRI's recommendation is that the silos between the intergovernmental system and other international governance actors would be reduced if the parallel forum provided a way for non-state communities to engage with the governing bodies of the UN system while they were designing new programs or promulgating soft law.

A parallel multistakeholder meeting track with an international body has a number of positive elements. It can be seen as a new form of standing multi-constituency consultation system where non-state actors provide advice and expertise to an intergovernmental body. It can also act to increase the acceptance of soft law decisions as governments collectively make the case for the soft law directly to key TNC executives. On the downside the parallel governance chamber system can function to provide negative pressure from non-state actors, particularly from powerful actors which do not want to change the status quo.

Replacement government in failed states

The GRI also recommends another structural form for multistakeholder governance. When national governments are seen as failing to govern their peoples adequately, GRI proposes that non-state actors join with international donors to manage these fragile states. GRI calls for:

> ... **a dual-oversight agency** where responsibility is shared between state authorities and external funders in order to meet the urgent needs of the population in fragile states through the delivery of essential social and economic services, while building sustainable and accountable systems of public authority.
>
> (WEF 2010: 14; bold in the original)

The rationale for this multistakeholder arrangement is really an extension of a PPP where the public-private partnership is not over a specific under-governed public space but over an under-governed country as a whole.

There are four unusual features for this proposed role of a multistakeholder group. First, it presumes that the government nominally in power is more legitimate than the forces opposing the government. In this sense the GRI proposal is giving political endorsement to apparent stability over what might be a more democratic and socially just oppositional force. Second, the external donors may refer to government aid agencies, private philanthropies, and foreign investors, all of which may be potentially connected to the cause of the failed state. Third, even if the external donors are not directly or indirectly responsible for the fragility of the governance system, there is little democratic basis for external funders to be part of a formal government. Donors may be able to provide resources of education, housing, health services, and related state activities, but they are inappropriate to be in government per se, which also has legislative, regulatory, and police powers. And finally, this recommendation explicitly proposes a multistakeholder national government when a country is declared to be a "fragile state," a classification that lacks a formal definition. Without a clear definition in international law, this proposed multistakeholder idea opens the prospect that donors, which have a significant economic or political interest in a territory, can use claims to the legitimacy of multistakeholderism to intervene in a conflict.

This proposal seems to be premised on the organizational belief that, if a current situation does not seem to have a solution under multilateralism, then maybe multistakeholderism is the way forward.

Chapter summary

The choice of the structure for a particular multistakeholder group is often the result of institutional compromises between competing claims for effectiveness, efficiency, and democratic legitimacy. The structures today are also the result of a dynamic global experimentation process on the forms and practices of multistakerholderism. The tension over these conflicting forces is often embedded in the way organizational beliefs influence the convener and key participants.

Internal battles over how to attract and then manage power differentials is reflected in organizational beliefs about the centrality of volunteerism for each participant and about the belief that a multistakeholder group can manage inter-and intra-category conflicts of interest. Governing councils with advisory chambers and those with weighted governing voting systems can be seen as institutionalizing a management system more centered on efficiency and effectiveness than one where there is an aspiration for a new global democratic system.

The organizational belief in a stakeholder-based global governance system is obviously central to a governance process termed "multistakeholderism." As with the generalization from citizens' rights to corporate personhood, this belief fundamentally shifts the terms of reference of a governance system. If being a "stakeholder" gives one the right to make global decisions, and being designated by a convener is the predominant way that one become certified as a relevant "stakeholder," then the gap between people, wherever they live, and the global governance system would become even wider under multistakeholderism than it was under multilateralism. The implication of a stakeholder-based governance system is explored further in Chapter 6.

The next chapter has a more limited goal. The chapter poses questions to assess the governance perspectives of specific multistakeholder undertakings, recognizing that these criteria will vary depending on the form of the proposed multistakeholder arrangement.

Notes

1 To make sure that a more diverse lead governing body does not try to oversee the dominant membership group, the lead body only functions in an advisory role to the Secretary-General.

2 See the following:

> The case studies exemplify a spectrum of decision-making procedures, ranging from consensus oriented deliberative approaches to a single point of unilateral control. This spectrum exists not just across case studies but within them, indicating that most groups utilize a range of procedures that are matched to the particular stage of the process and the context.... Other case studies describe groups that begin with consensus procedures but switch to other approaches as necessary.
>
> (Gasser et al. 2015: 13)

3 For example, see the analyses by Raymond and DeNardis (2015) and Dingwerth (2007).
4 See: www.everywomaneverychild.org/about/.
5 See: www.se4all.org/.

References

Adam, Lishan, Tina James, and Munyua Wanjira. 2007. "Frequently asked questions about multi-stakeholder partnerships in ICTs for development: A guide for national ICP policy animators." Melville, South Africa: Association for Progressive Communications.

Alliance for Responsible Mining. n.d. "Board of Directors." Accessed January 10, 2018. Available from www.responsiblemines.org/en/who-we-are/board-of-directors/.

Asmal, Kader. 2001. "Introduction: World Commission on Dams Report. Dams and Development." *American University International Law Review* 16, no. 6: 1411–33.

Dingwerth, Klaus. 2007. *The New Transnationalism: Transnational Governance and Democratic Legitimacy*. Basingstoke: Palgrave Macmillan.

Dingwerth, Klaus and Philipp Pattberg. 2009. "World Politics and Organizational Fields: The Case of Transnational Sustainability Governance." *European Journal of International Relations* 15, no. 4: 707–44.

Gasser, Urs, Ryan Budish and Sarah West. 2015. "Multistakeholder as Governance Groups: Observations from Case Studies." Cambridge, MA: Berkman Klein Center, Harvard University.

Global Coffee Platform. n.d. "Governance." Accessed January 5, 2018. Introduction: Available from www.globalcoffeeplatform.com/about/governance.

Global Compact. 2013. "Terms of Reference: Global Compact Board Members." Last modified April 22, 2013. Available from www.unglobalcompact.org/docs/about_the_gc/Terms_of_Reference_Board.pdf.

Global Partnership for Effective Development Co-operation. 2017. "2017 and 2018 Programme of Work." Washington DC: Global Partnership for Effective Development Co-operation.

Global Water Partnership. 2017. "What is the Network?" Last modified May 18, 2017. Available from www.gwp.org/en/About/who/What-is-the-network/.

ICANN. 2012. "Governance Guidelines. Last modified October 18, 2012. Available from www.icann.org/resources/pages/guidelines-2012-05-15-en.

ICANN. 2014. "ICANN Strategic Plan for fiscal years 2016–2020." Los Angeles, CA: Internet Corporation for Assigned Names and Numbers. Available from www.icann.org/en/system/files/files/strategic-plan-2016-2020-10oct14-en.pdf.

ISS. 2010. *Global Governance 2025: At a Critical Juncture*. Paris: The European Union Institute for Security Studies.

Joshi, Sachin. 2016. "Privatization of Global Governance." Stockholm: The Global Challenges Foundation.

Raymond, Mark, and Laura DeNardis. 2015. "Multistakeholderism: anatomy of an inchoate global institution." *International Theory* 7, no. 3: 572–616.

Pattberg, Philipp. 2012. *Public-private Partnerships for Sustainable Development: Emergence, Influence and Legitimacy*. Cheltenham: Edward Elgar Publishing.

UN. 2008. *Towards Global Partnerships: on the report of the Second Committee (A/62/426)*. GA Agenda Item 61, UN GA 62nd session, UN Doc Res A/RES/62/211 (distributed March 11, 2008; adopted December 19, 2007).

UN. 2015a. *Towards Global Partnerships: a principle-based approach to enhanced cooperation between the United Nations and all relevant partners*. GA Agenda Item 27, UN GA 70th session, UN Doc A/RES/70/224 (distributed February 23, 2016; adopted December 22, 2015).

UN. 2015b. *Transforming our World: the 2030 Agenda for Sustainable Development*, GA Res 70/1, UN GA 70th session, UN Doc A/RES/70/1 (October 21, 2015; adopted September 25, 2015).

Vallejo, Nancy and Pierre Hauselmann. 2004. "Governance and Multi-stakeholder Processes" Winnipeg, Canada: United Nations Conference on Trade and Development, the International Institute for Sustainable Development, and the Swiss State Secretariat for Economic Affairs.

WEF. 2010. "Everyone's Business: Strengthening International Cooperation in a More Interdependent World: Report of the Global Redesign Initiative." Geneva: World Economic Forum.

World Ocean Council. n.d. "Partnerships and Key Stakeholders." Accessed November 28, 2017. Available from www.oceancouncil.org/about-us/accreditations/.

5 A detailed guide to decision-making about a multistakeholder group

Multistakeholderism poses a different set of management and governance challenges than other international governance systems. To assist in decision-making about multistakeholder groups (MSGs), this chapter offers a practical guide based around a series of rhetorical questions that can be used to appraise an MSG at the micro and practical level. It has three different potential uses. In the first instance, it is intended to contribute from a bottom-up perspective to the overall assessment of the democratic characteristics of multistakeholderism. Second, it is intended to provide a tool to appraise the currently operating experimental MSGs to evaluate their democratic integrity. And third, it offers a series of questions to help organizational leaders, public policy researchers, students of global institutions, and citizens assess if they should accept an invitation to join a specific MSG or to endorse an MSG as the preferred way to deliver a specific public good.

In some cases, the expected efficiency and effectiveness of a multistakeholder proposal may well override governance concerns. This is likely to occur, for instance, if a short-term crisis looms and there is no international agency or leading group of governments prepared to act expeditiously; or if a long-term crisis has continued without a significant international movement to resolve it. In these and other cases, a new configuration of actors outside the multilateral system may be the best route to kick start a solution to an issue. Sometimes, it appears that getting attention from enthusiastic, powerful actors to a global problem could be good for democracy. While other studies have provided guidance on how to assess and build the effectiveness or efficiency of a specific MSG (Hemmati et al. 2002; UN 2013; Brouwer et al. 2016; WEF 2016; ISEAL 2017), this chapter focus exclusively on the governance aspects of MSGs.

In management terms there are three distinct decision points for assessing the democratic practices of an individual MSG. The first decision point is obviously in the planning and initiation phase of an MSG. At this point, organizational leaders and potential participants ought to ask themselves if the governance structure for a proposed MSG aligns with their organizational principles or if they consider that the public good should better be delivered in another fashion. The second decision point is an annual or pre-determined multi-year review moment when the multistakeholder participants can self-assess how things are going and/or can invite wider comments from the affected public. The closure process of the MSG, as is usual in the creation of a corporate partnership, should also be agreed at the outset. The founding papers should specify how the project should end, if all goes well, and what happens if things do not go well. The third decision point then centers on the process which should occur when an MSG is ending, either because the group completed its task or the group partially or completely collapsed.

From a democratic governance perspective, the relevance of the initial decision point is rather obvious. The second decision point – the review moment – has three sub-components: (a) a review within the organizations taking part in a specific MSG to determine if their participation continues to align with their institutional goals; (b) a self-reflective review component by the whole MSG – a moment to take stock of how things are working from a governance perspective as well as the overall continued soundness of the terms of reference; and (c) a different moment when the community concerned about a given topic is encouraged to share with the MSG their assessment of how the MSG is contributing (or not) to managing a given topic. All review assessments should be well-documented in order to make subsequent reviews meaningful as well as to provide a sound set of working papers for newer members of the MSG.

The third decision point – planning for closure – should lay out how to address some difficult issues, such as what steps members should take when they individually or collectively think that the group should be shuttered, what happens with the assets, liabilities, and the name of the MSG after a planned or unexpected demise, and what explanations should be publicly available about the rationale behind the departure of key organizational participants and the rationale others might have to see the group continue.

The rhetorical questions in this chapter are organized around four democratic aspects of the governance of a multistakeholder project: (a) the composition of the MSG; (b) the standards used for internal governance; (c) the accountability and outreach to external communities; and (d) financial matters. The commentary on each question opens with a review of how that topic is usually handled in democratic nations and in multilateralism. As noted earlier, these two systems are used as a comparative baseline to assess the relative depth of democracy in any given MSG, not because they are a gold standard about how democracy ought to function. After the commentary on each question, there is a section on basic democratic practices that should reasonably be expected from an MSG. While the questions and the commentary are neutrally formulated, the basic governance criteria are intentionally prescriptive but are not intended to be comprehensive. They have been inspired by the thinking of a number of different authors (Global Knowledge Partnership 2003; UNECE 2008; Martens 2007; MSI 2015, 2017; WHO 2003, 2017).

Four questions on the composition of a multistakeholder group

The first group of questions addresses the membership of the governing body of an MSG. Specifically, the section raises questions about the appropriate categories of participants for a given multistakeholder governance group; the due diligence criteria that should be considered for organizations and individuals; the selection process for identifying organizations from each stakeholder category including the process within each organization to select the individual to act on its behalf; and, finally, the diversity practices within an MSG. The actual process is often not as clearly sequential as reflected in the questions below.

Over time, members of a given MSG may withdraw or new members be recruited. These four questions on the composition of an MSG should be re-examined whenever there is a change in membership, particularly because the departure or addition of designated stakeholders may significantly alter the internal balance of power and the perceived external authority of an MSG.

#1 Are all the appropriate categories of participants reflected in the multistakeholder group?

In a democracy, various methods are used to aggregate citizen views into legitimate representative bodies. Primaries, party caucuses, and direct elections are amongst the ways that representation is given clear and public legitimacy. The multilateral system is built around governments and the intergovernmental organizations created by governments. The core democratic credo of multilateralism is one-country-one-vote.

In multistakeholderism, as the name itself implies, there are multiple categories of governance actors. The toughest issue is identifying all the relevant upstream and downstream communities that may be affected by the group's decisions and providing them with an equal opportunity to influence the direction of the MSG. In many cases, when approached to support or participate in an MSG, the first reaction of a stakeholder is to consider whether their category or sector is represented. As discussed in Chapter 3, the convener is often given an unduly free hand in defining the relevant categories of stakeholders, knowing that potential new members may be more concerned that there is space for their stakeholder category and thus being insufficiently attentive to the inclusion or exclusion of the other categories of stakeholders. This leaves the convener with a strong hand in selecting the balance of stakeholder categories.

114 *Decisions around multistakeholder groups*

Some stakeholder categories might signal that they want to be part of an MSG whereas other stakeholder categories, like those most likely to be affected, are more likely to be under-informed about the plans for the MSG, or they might have a high level of difficulty simply participating in a given MSG. Therefore which stakeholder categories are included – or excluded – from an MSG can largely determine the opportunities for success – or the limitation of the results – of the entire effort.

The definitional boundaries of stakeholder categories and the management of a proliferation of categories of stakeholders is a democratic challenge for all engaged with an MSG. For further analysis on the ability to identify all relevant stakeholders and proposed solutions to winnow down the number of categories, see Chapter 4.

Basic democratic practices that should be expected:

a   *Access to information* – Members of each potential stakeholder category should be able to receive a list of proposed stakeholder categories and the definitions used to define these stakeholder categories.
b   *Ability to challenge stakeholder categories* – Each multistakeholder governance group should have a platform to argue for the inclusion or exclusion of any other stakeholder category.
c   *Conflict of interest exclusions* – Stakeholder categories that might financially benefit from the outcome of a particular MSG should be presumed inappropriate members of that governance group.
d   *Restrictions on more powerful stakeholders* – The more economically, militarily, or socially powerful members of an MSG ought not to have the power to directly select or veto selections of other stakeholder categories.
e   *Inclusion of the most affected or impacted communities and constituencies* – Each MSG should include organizations and social movements which may face the greatest consequence from the activities of the MSG.

#2 What internationally recognized criteria should be used to select a legitimate organization to represent a stakeholder category or to select an individual representative within these organizations?

The political credibility of the whole MSG rests on the least morally clear or the most publicly discredited participant. Internationally recognized moral and policy criteria statements are ideal tools to screen potential stakeholder categories and individual members of an MSG.

All TNCs and all CSOs, to select just two potential categories of stakeholders, are not blemish-free. TNCs routinely examine their business and government partners when they approve supply contracts, undertake due diligence for mergers, and make long-term commitments with high visibility customers. The governance question for multistakeholderism is how to conduct similar due diligence reviews for stakeholder categories and for individuals who might participate in governance roles.

There can be positive and negative criteria for the selection of organizations from a given stakeholder category and the subsequent selection of individuals from within an organization. On the positive side, some organizations in a stakeholder category may have already publicly acknowledged the importance of an issue and are seen by the wider public as having a crucial and early role in defining the scope of that issue. On the negative side, some organizations might have such a strong interest in a particular outcome (e.g., anti-abortion or anti-vaccines groups participating in a health MSG) that their participation would harm the overall goal of the MSG. Other organizations which may be under indictment or investigation or have a significantly tarnished public reputation may be excluded in order to avoid potential negative publicity.

Basic democratic practices that should be expected:

a *A pre-establishment procedure* – Before an MSG formally starts, each proposed stakeholder should have an opportunity for a proper due diligence review of the other candidate members of the MSG.
b *Positive selection criteria* – These criteria ought to include as accepted (1) key human rights principles from the UN Human Rights Council; (2) the Sustainable Development Goals adopted by the General Assembly; (3) the core labor standards developed by the ILO; (4) the environmental and climate change goals adopted in international conventions and agreements; as well as (5) other intergovernmental goals that are particularly related to the topic of the MSG.
c *Negative selection criteria* – These criteria ought to include that a group or individual member (1) is not under indictment or been convicted of financial, criminal, civil or moral crimes; (2) is not seen as working against a Security Council decision; and (3) is not involved in trafficking of persons, weapons, or banned products or inciting racial, gender, religious or ethnic hatred.
d *Minimization of conflicts of interest* – Each multistakeholder governance group should have a clear conflict of interest policy statement that includes (1) that any participant using the MSG for market-oriented self-interest make available a market impact statement regarding the potential benefits from participating in the MSG; (2) that all financial transactions within the MSG and with individual participants are fully and regularly disclosed; (3) that prior professional or occupational relationships between organizations and individual participants are made publicly available; and (4) that a public process is established to evaluate any reported potential conflicts of interest.

e   *A periodic post-establishment procedure* – The MSG should schedule periodic reviews to candidly address ethical and political concerns about an organization's or individual stakeholder's actions that arise after the formation of the group.

#3 How should an organization be designated for each stakeholder category and how should individuals be selected to represent each participating organization?

In multilateral systems of governance, the head of government of a nation-state designates directly or indirectly the section of government to participate in international governance activities. The head of that governmental office then designates directly or indirectly the individual to represent that office at an international event.

Under multistakeholderism, no major stakeholder category has a legitimate representative body which can use its internal decision-making capacity to designate a proper representative to serve on a multistakeholder governance body. On the other hand, almost every significant stakeholder category can well make a claim that they should be part of any global policy-making MSG. And a good number of stakeholder categories can be quite politically worried if they were excluded from key public-private project MSGs and key global standard-setting MSGs.

In practice, selection criteria to designate an organization to represent a category of stakeholders can include the degree of access to power within the category, the extent of power of that organization to influence institutions and events outside the MSG, the probability that an organization might contribute financially to the operation of the group, the organization's potential receptiveness to the final outcome preferred by the founders, and whether an organization can provide a protective barrier to a hostile external community. Similar selection criteria may apply to the selection of individuals on their own or as the representative of a given organization. For example, a faculty member from a well-regarded university may be included to protect the MSG from criticism about its scientific assumptions.

Participants that represent an organization within the designated stakeholder category are seldom, if ever, designated by a decision of their corporate board, NGO board of directors, labor union council, or the membership of the organization. The two dominant ways of designating individuals to represent an organization are (a) the convener extending an invitation to an individual to participate in the MSG, leaving the organizational approval process up to that individual; or (b) the staff leadership of an organization tasking a team member to participate in the multistakeholder governance body. In each of these cases, the organization continues to provide salary and possibly costs of participation, but in neither case does the formal governance arrangement of the sponsoring organization play an active role in designating the appropriate person or setting the policy guidelines and reporting requirements for that individual.

For both the selection of organizations designated to represent a stakeholder category and for the designation of individuals to represent these organizations, the internal and on-going consultation processes within stakeholder categories and within the sponsoring organization are very important. If that organization is to be the contact for that stakeholder category, then there should be an arrangement established to inquire of other members of that stakeholder group regarding their views on the appropriateness of the MSG and whether the organization originally approached by a convener is the most appropriate organization to be a participant in the MSG. If there is an agreement to go forward, the organization designated to be the intermediary should also seek to develop a consensus-based position on policy and program directions to take to the MSG. Similarly, if an individual within an organization is given the responsibility and potential liability to participate in an MSG, then the sponsoring organization should have a clear supervisory structure and a clear ability to recall individuals who might be operating outside of their instructions.

Basic democratic practices that should be expected:

a   *Participant pre-approval from one's own organization* – Each participant and an alternative participant should have formal permission from their organization's governing body to work with a multistakeholder body.
b   *Right of stakeholder groups to appoint their own representatives* – The right of each stakeholder group to appoint its own representatives independently and free from coercion by other stakeholder categories and the convener should be explicitly guaranteed.
c   *Removal of a participant* – Each organization, upon the decision of its members or through its own independent process, should be able to replace its representatives in the MSG at any time following its own governance mechanisms.
d   *Continuing obligation to consult with one's designated community* – A designee or representative of a stakeholder category should establish a procedure for regular consultation with key members of that stakeholder category and for reporting back to that community.

#4 What should be the overall diversity balance for a multistakeholder group?

In multilateralism, geographic balance in staff recruitment, public panels, and intergovernmental committees is an accepted practice. Each level of staff and each intergovernmental body is designed to have a geopolitical balance. The UN definition of geopolitical balance was crafted during the period of decolonization and during the Cold War and, as such, no longer reflects contemporary geopolitical realities.[1] While gender balance in these areas is accepted in principle, it is not as routinely followed in practice as geographic diversity. In addition, the multilateral system has not addressed the full range of important diversity governance issues, such as representation based on age, ethnicity, indigenous national status, or economic class.

Ensuring diversity in global governance is far more complicated in multistakeholderism than it is in multilateralism. Broadly speaking, there are three possibilities: each multistakeholder category in an MSG is diversity-balanced; the balance is achieved across the MSG taking into account the diversity imbalance of each stakeholder category; or the designee for each stakeholder category "doubles" as a representative of a different diversity community. Each of these approaches is in tension with membership selection based on the appropriate inclusion of "stakeholders" as the guiding membership criterion.

The first approach toward addressing this tension taken by some MSGs, which have made an explicit commitment to diversity, is to have a quota system or a designated seat at the table for each specific diversity community. Leaving aside how a specific diversity community is included or excluded from having its designated seat, it means that the ratio of the diversity community presence to the overall group would be one out of the total number of individuals in the MSG; hardly an arrangement for an effective voice for that diversity community.

Alternatively, if each stakeholder category is to be constructed with a sensitivity to multiple vectors of diversity, then each stakeholder category either needs to have a number of individuals equal to the number of diversity communities that are considered significant, or a way to select individuals who in their own history or self-identification can be said to be associated with multiple social or cultural identities. In the former situation, the size of the MSG would multiply by the number of diversity communities considered relevant; in the latter situation, the pool of prospective members of the group would be significantly narrowed to those individuals who belong to a designated stakeholder category and who happen to offer a specific combination of other relevant identities.

Aligning a stakeholder-based selection system with one that is diversity balanced is a challenging democratic endeavor.

Basic democratic practices that ought to be expected:

a   *Diversity principle* – Each MSG should ensure that the overall combination of designees in the governing body and in the separate chambers is balanced at the minimum on gender, ethnicity, and geopolitical terms.
b   *Diversity disclosure* – Each organizational body needs to disclose the definitions used for each diversity group and the number of members of that group in the body.

Decisions around multistakeholder groups 119

c   *Non-diversity correction* – If any governing body or chamber does not meet the diversity principles, it should disclose a plan and a timetable for remedying that situation.
d   *Diversity review* – There needs to be regular review on an agreed pre-arranged schedule of the diversity balance and the degree of effective voice for each diversity community.

Four questions on internal governance

In multilateralism, the rule books and informal governance processes are designed to create an ambiance for meaningful discussion and effective decision-making while managing asymmetric capacities between governments. Multistakeholderism needs similar rule books. As there are multiple types of institutional decision-makers, each with their own form of capacity and power, the formal and informal internal governance processes would need to address a wider range of procedural, politically sensitive, and relative power concerns. For example, documents and working languages for MSG meetings should not presume that everyone is fluent in English or French. And a simple traditional concept like quorum may well need a special definition to reflect an adequate proportion of each stakeholder group in order to meet the minimal condition of a quorum.

This section addresses the basic process of deciding what the MSG will do, how the group is going to do this, and how to handle differences of views.

#1 Are the terms of reference for the group clear and acceptable?

Framing a global issue is generally considered the first step in a political process. Debates over the terms of reference occur because the control over the definition of a problem often gives a lead to – or places a restriction on – the likely outcome of the overall effort. The terms of reference can – explicitly or implicitly – also provide a basis for commitments, obligations, or responsibilities that may flow from the final outcome of a process.

In intergovernmental fora, governments often spend considerable amounts of time negotiating the wording used to frame an issue. Sometimes this ends up in a lengthy resolution reflecting compromises between diverse viewpoints. On other occasions, it results in an ambiguous phrase or a section that keeps a particularly complex issue open for future negotiations.

The terms of reference for a multistakeholder body are equally important for both the potential participants in the MSG and those who may be affected by the actions of the multistakeholder project. For participants and potential participants in a multistakeholder project, the Bali Principles Governing the Management of Multistakeholder ICT Partnerships for Sustainable Development provide a straightforward statement on the importance of such terms of reference:

Consensus should be sought for a written document identifying, at a minimum: the shared vision of the partnership, the objectives of each partner for the partnership, and the division of roles and responsibilities.

(Global Knowledge Partnership 2003)

It is important to assess what is included in the scope of work and what appears to be excluded from the scope of work. For example, GoodWeave's terms of reference demonstrate a commitment "to stop child labor in the carpet industry and to replicate its market-based approach in other sectors" (GoodWeave n.d.). With this scoping statement, proposed solutions are intentionally restricted to market-based interventions and similarly against legally binding solutions. The terms of reference of the International Code of Conduct for Private Security Providers states its goal as being "to articulate human rights responsibilities of private security companies (PSCs), and to set out international principles and standards for the responsible provision of private security services, particularly when operating in complex environments" (ICoCA n.d.). Clearly, the goal to articulate standards is designed to exclude the MSG from engaging in actions in any actual armed conflict, labelled here a "complex environment."

Often, the convening of an MSG is done with only vague terms of reference – sometimes just 5–10 words, such as: "address the crisis caused by X," or, "do something about problem Y."[2] Other times, the terms of reference include a call phrased in the development vocabulary of the day such as to "support the SDGs," the "Paris climate conference," or "women's rights." This call seldom clarifies which aspects of these broad assertions the MSG itself is planning to solve or how the MSG may or may not actually coordinate its work with the intergovernmental body that initiated the developmental aspiration.

Such levels of ambiguity can exacerbate the asymmetries of power within the MSG, as different participants can understand the goal in fundamentally different ways (see Chapter 4). Further, they make it difficult for a potential organizational stakeholder or individual to make a sound political judgement about affiliating in some way with a given multistakeholder governance group.

For those who may be affected by the actions of an MSG, there are three other levels of potential concern. First, do the proposed terms of reference for the MSG unnecessarily minimize or weaken existing multilateral bodies or other international organizations by shifting the locus of decision-making out of a public process to a more restricted space? Second, do the terms of reference adequately assure that conflicts of interest can be handled appropriately and are subject to public disclosure and review? Third, do the terms of reference have the effect of excluding social constituencies that should be participating in the MSG or excluding solutions that should be given appropriate attention?

Basic democratic practices that should be expected:

a   *Avoidance of language barriers* – Language(s) used in meetings, terms of reference, and working publications should not be a barrier for effective participation.
b   *Openness to potential and current stakeholders* – The deliberation process regarding terms of reference and any review of the terms of reference should allow opportunities to liaise with potential stakeholders inside the group as well as with stakeholders outside of the group to ensure that (1) it is transparently and legitimately in concert with all potential stakeholders and (2) it addresses all stakeholders' concerns regarding an MSG's internal governance.
c   *For standard-setting multistakeholder groups* – The terms of reference should include the definition of the market involved; the basic principles that will be used to determine the criteria for a "good" product or service in that market; the criteria for certifying or supervising the certification of the "good" product or service; and the process of selecting and verifying the implementation of the criteria for particular products and services.
d   *Nature of obligations, responsibilities, and potential liabilities* – The terms of reference should define the nature of the obligations, responsibilities, and potential liabilities for the multistakeholder project as a whole and for the organizations and individuals affiliated with the MSG as well as any formal and informal relationships with the UN system.
e   *Modification of terms of reference* – The published terms of reference should describe the pre-arranged timetable for their review and how they may be modified by members of the MSG.

#2 How will decision-making operate within the multistakeholder group?

For almost all UN system governing bodies there are formal rules, informal rules, and unwritten rules. Over the past twenty-five years, experimentation with new rules and practices has become commonplace.

These formal and informal rules grew out of years of intergovernmental negotiations and the evolution of international law. Some are codified in the rule books of the United Nations system organizations and others, particularly the unwritten rules, are woven into the culture of each intergovernmental body.

In the evolving multistakeholder system there are no recognized standards governing the internal decision-making process of the three types of MSGs. Over time, there may be an agreed common rule book and set of practices. Dingwerth and Pattberg argue that this is occurring in environmental and social standard-setting MSGs, as each new group shares

122 *Decisions around multistakeholder groups*

isomorphic practices and structures with pre-existing groups (Dingwerth and Pattberg 2009).

Some multistakeholder governance groups work with a high degree of internal confidentiality about their decision-making rules. For example, neither the agenda nor the outcome of meetings of the World Economic Forum's Global Future Councils are public. With notable exceptions, MSGs do not tend to publish their internal governance processes and rule books on their websites. The rules on decision-making can institutionalize pre-existing imbalances of power or act as a counter-balance to the dominance of those with disproportionate external power. As such, the absence of a good, clear rule book and understanding of the informal practices can make it difficult to make a sound judgement about the democratic acceptability of any given MSG.

Basic democratic practices that should be expected:

a   *Ensure the operational rules are agreed by unanimity* – However the rules are drafted, the published final working rule book must be confirmed by consensus agreement of all MSG members. Its publication contributes to ensuring that non-member stakeholders perceive the governance processes of the MSGs as more credible and predictable.

b   *Core elements* – A good rule book ought to include: (1) the method for the selection of the chair; (2) the length of terms for the chair and other members; (3) the method for adopting decisions; (4) the method for objecting to the adoption of a decision; (5) the rules regarding the minimum number of participants from each stakeholder category to hold a meeting; (6) the procedure to review hiring and retaining staff; (7) the conditions under which the chair, staff, or members can speak on behalf of the group; (8) the procedures to revise the number of stakeholder categories, representative organizations, or key individuals; (9) the duration of a member's mandate and term limits; (10) the circulation of pending decisions; (11) the arrangements for publishing and circulating minority statements; (12) the methods for organizations and individuals to depart from the organization; and (13) the method for closing the MSG.

c   *A process to hold members and their organizations accountable* – The terms of reference and/or the rule books should include procedures for reviewing and sanctioning members for inadequate performance of their duties, including the authority to revoke membership or request a replacement individual – either by the voluntary decision of the stakeholder group or by consensus agreement of the whole MSG – as well as the procedures for organizations and individuals to stand down when specific decisions may represent – or may be perceived to represent – a conflict of interest.

#3 What should be the dispute resolution system for a multistakeholder group?

In those countries with parliamentary systems, members of parliament can raise a question to the prime minister or foreign minister asking them to explain a government position and, if they are not satisfied, they can bring an action that can prompt the government to re-open an issue. In other situations, citizens can use the national courts, administrative tribunals, or legislative hearings to challenge a government's implementation of its laws and regulations.

In the multilateral system, governments can challenge a ruling by the chair, argue that a given subject should be considered in another intergovernmental body, appeal to the legal counsel's office for a ruling, interrupt a debate when it feels that its fundamental rights are being questioned, and submit written or oral minority statements or permanent reservations to conventions. In addition, non-state constituencies which disagree with an intergovernmental action can protest directly to that intergovernmental body or its international secretariat.

Formal dispute resolution procedures are an under-developed governance structure for multistakeholderism. It is not that similar concerns faced by multilateral body do not exist for multistakeholderism, but that to the extent that a given MSG asserts that all stakeholders are represented, it seems to regard the democratic necessity to hear challenges to decisions and actions as unnecessary. This is particularly difficult when the challenge is that the organization has stepped outside its terms of reference, is not implementing its terms of reference, or has taken a policy or programmatic direction that may be perceived as antithetical to the views of a given member or a non-member.

As MSI Integrity (2015: 79) stated in its study of EITI:

> These mechanisms can protect the internal trust of the [stakeholder group] by ensuring that disputes are resolved through a predictable and procedurally fair process agreed by all stakeholders before disputes arise. They preserve the public legitimacy of the MSG by offering an accessible avenue for concerned citizens to engage the decision-making body responsible for implementing the EITI and seek remedies for substantive concerns or misconduct related to aspects of EITI implementation.

Basic democratic practices that should be expected:

a   *A grievance mechanism for internal matters* – An established dispute resolution mechanism should allow members of the MSG to address grievances related to internal governance rules, breaches of member responsibilities, and forms of discrimination, internal harassment, and conflicts of interest.

b *A grievance mechanism for external challenges* – An open platform should be constructed to receive information on breaches of the multistakeholder governance rules and procedures, grievances related to public complaints regarding substantive compliance and impacts of the MSG, allegations of misconduct by multistakeholder members, under-evaluated consequences of a multistakeholder action or non-action, and insufficiency of the organization's reporting process.

c *Predictable, fair, and legitimate grievance rules* – Good grievance rules ought to include: (1) eligibility qualifications for who can file or report grievances, and on what grounds complaints may be reported; (2) accessible procedures for reporting grievances or complaints; (3) eligibility qualifications for evaluators of complaints, such as procedures for appointing adjudicators or tribunals; (4) a procedure for minority opinions on grievance matters; and, (5) transparency rules regarding how and when complaints should be published, the reasoning behind the decisions, and (6) the actions taken by the MSG, the member organizations or individuals based on the outcome of the grievance process.

#4 What procedures should be followed to decide to close a multistakeholder group?

Closing an MSG, like shuttering any organization, can be a painful process. There will always be competing claims by some participants as to whether it is appropriate or necessary to have a planned closure. And there will be frictions or even possibly court cases if the closure is unplanned and un-thought out. Consequently, as with any corporate partnership, the founding documents and the terms of reference should address what should happen when the MSG finishes its work or elects for any number of reasons to terminate its efforts.

Writing these closure rules in advance is difficult. It is even more difficult when there is pressure for closure and there are no pre-agreed procedures. Whenever there is a scheduled periodic review of the governance of the MSG, it is appropriate to take a second look at the pre-agreed procedures for closure and the conditions that might make closure a reasonable and timely choice.

Basic democratic practices that should be expected:

a *Proceeding to closure* – The grounds for requesting an internal discussion for the dissolution of an MSG should be made clear. As some members of the MSG might feel that any discussion of closure would undermine the future viability of the MSG, a clear statement on the basis for a discussion of termination should be a part of any sound management plan.

b *Unplanned withdrawals of a stakeholder category* – Unless there is a procedure in place to re-appoint these stakeholders, an unplanned

withdrawal of key stakeholders, particularly the complete withdrawal of a whole category of stakeholders, should prompt a formal review of the terms of reference and operating practice of the MSG.
c *Financial matters* – The closure plan or the arrangement for unplanned closure should include how to handle organizational assets, cover the organizational commitments to staff and other contractors, and how to meet any incurred liabilities.

Three questions on external responsibilities

This section looks at the engagement of members of an MSG with their organizational sponsor, with other organizations in the same stakeholder category, with multilateralism, and with the wider society. It also addresses the nature of the responsibilities, liabilities, and obligations that may flow from participating in an MSG.

#1 How should an organization in a multistakeholder group engage with others in its designated stakeholder group and how should an individual participant engage with her/his organization?

In multilateralism, there is an intra-governmental coordination process and an inter-governmental negotiation process. At the government delegation level, representatives of a government coordinate with the local ambassador, with their foreign ministry, and sometimes with one of their national specialized government agencies. A delegation also consults and negotiates with other governments in their geopolitical group, with governments which share a common interest in a given topic, and with the international secretariat for a particular intergovernmental body.

Were a government official asked to participate in an MSG, that official would seek authorization from her/his agency before replying. The government agency's assessment would involve an appraisal of the benefits to the government from the potential success – or failure – of the MSG. The agency would also assess the budgetary costs of government-supported staff time and related expenditures to participate effectively in a particular MSG. It is also likely to assess the risks and benefits for the government from publicly joining with specific TNCs, CSOs, and other governments and participants to tackle a task.

As a non-state participant in global governance, many of the same issues apply to non-state actors but in a more complicated manner. In terms of engagement with other organizations in their designated stakeholder group, the non-state organization would need to evaluate whether it shares with an MSG the same conceptual definition of its designated stakeholder group. If so, is it expected to consult with other organizations in its stakeholder category? The latter standard is difficult, as other organizations in

126 *Decisions around multistakeholder groups*

the stakeholder group may be geographically distant and some are direct organizational competitors. The leadership of the organization and the individual selected to participate in the MSG also need to appraise whether consultation would be limited to the decision to join or support a particular MSG, or whether the consultation process will be an on-going reality with a scheduled timetable.

For the internal consultation process, the non-state organization has to appraise whether the existing organizational reporting process is appropriate, whether it should establish a formal internal management review process to supervise its staff involvement, or whether this engagement oversight should be elevated to the governing body or membership of the organization. As with government participation, non-state organizations have to determine if they are in a position to provide the time and resources for their participation in the group and in any external consultation processes.

Lawyers, accountants, academics, religious leaders, and other professionals serving on an MSG are in a functionally different position, but they too could well consider the appropriateness of consultation with their professional colleagues and related professional associations.

Basic democratic practices that should be expected:

a *Public stakeholder comment practice* – Each participating organization should host a distinct page on its website with information on their role in each MSG they choose to join, the issues the organization sees to be of relevance to its stakeholder category, and a comment function for concerned members of the public to share their views on positions taken and on possible future directions for the MSG.
b *Constituency stakeholder consultation practice* – Each participating organization should convene on a regular basis with other organizations in the stakeholder group to review the developments for their stakeholder group and to seek guidance on upcoming policy and programmatic issues.
c *Internal organizational review* – Each participating organization should schedule regular internal reviews of the issues confronting the stakeholder groups that it participates in, the policy and programmatic consequences for its organization and others in the stakeholder group, and the success or difficulties faced by staff member in that process.
d *Continuing obligation of participants to their organization* – A designee or representative should be given instructions before a meeting and report afterwards to their appropriate organizational leaders.[3]

#2 What should be the reporting and disclosure standards to the general public and the multilateral system?

In national democracies, there are generally rules governing the types of documents that are mandated to be freely available, a timetable for the pre-publication for comment of draft government actions, and procedures to allow citizens to demand the release of non-confidential internal working papers.

In multilateralism, disclosure and reporting about intergovernmental activities and the work of the related secretariats takes many forms. In some cases, this is done by the secretariat releasing meeting documents and research papers; in other cases, the chair of an intergovernmental body submits a statement to a higher-level intergovernmental body.

For multistakeholderism, there are significant upsides and downsides to a formal reporting system to multilateral institutions and to the general public. Gasser et al. (2015: 15) summarize well the upside of a sound reporting system:

> External communication helps outside observers understand the process and outcome, ultimately helping build support for the work of the group and enhancing the perceived legitimacy of the outcome. When successful, communication (often enabled by Internet technologies) can even extend the breadth and depth of participation in the process itself, enabling far-flung interactions and creating a multidirectional communications stream.

Multistakeholder bodies often fault governments and other institutions because they lack transparency and accountability. However, multistakeholder bodies themselves have a mixed record on transparency and accountability. Multistakeholder bodies seldom publish policy documents or action plans in draft or have the equivalent of a freedom-of-information system. The irony of this two-sided practice may come about because multistakeholder bodies assert that all relevant stakeholders are incorporated inside the group and consequently they, as a multistakeholder project, do not need to reach out to other communities or institutions when they are formulating policies or plans.

For policy-oriented MSGs, it is particularly relevant whether the MSG intends to work autonomously or is formally committed to reporting on its activities to a relevant intergovernmental body. In the latter case, participants should reasonably want to know the nature of the relationship with the intergovernmental body, who will be the interlocutor with the intergovernmental organization, how reports from the MSG will be approved, and how the reaction of the intergovernmental body will influence the next phase of the MSG.

Basic democratic practices that should be expected:

a   *Transparency* – Establish the presumption of transparency for a group's processes, budgets, records, and decisions.
b   *Disclosure of membership and staff* – Require that current member and staff lists are made publicly available, including members' names,

organizational affiliation, the stakeholder group they represent, and the best method for contacting these members.

c *Open meeting rules* – Establish that meetings are open to the public by default. Where requests to observe meetings are denied, require a public explanation for the policy decision to prohibit attendance.

d *Access to minutes* – Arrange that meeting minutes are available to the public promptly after being finalized. Meeting minutes should include, at a minimum, an attendance list of meeting participants and any absent multistakeholder members; a copy of the agenda of issues to be discussed; and outcomes for all issues decided at the meeting and, where possible, reasons for the decisions. This includes instances where consensus could not be reached or votes did not pass, and identification of members that abstained from, or disagreed with, the decision.

e *Exceptions and confidentiality* – Pre-establish if there are grounds for any exceptions to the presumption of transparency and explain the legitimate policy reasons or circumstances for confidentiality around a discussion, decision, meeting, financial transaction or record.

#3 How should the multistakeholder group engage with the wider community on closure or a potential closure?

Public-private partnerships (PPPs), environmental and social standard-setting MSGs, and high-impact standard-setting groups create a complex dynamic with many actors that are upstream and downstream of the terms of reference of the MSG. These other actors may have allocated capital and time to the MSG on the assumption that the standard-setting process would be stable or that the public-private partnership would be meeting its declared goals. In some cases, communities and entire sub-economic sectors may well have altered long-standing social, political, or economic arrangements to adapt to a PPP or an international multistakeholder standard-setting body and need to begin a public process to adapt to the changed circumstances.

For planned closures, those organizations and communities impacted by the MSG could well benefit from a solid appraisal for why an MSG chooses to withdraw from its global governance role.

Basic democratic practices that should be expected:

a *Forewarning* – Establish the presumption that as part of any closure of an MSG that may have social, political, or financial ripple effects on communities, economic sectors, or states, these communities, economic sectors, and states are provided with adequate, timely and direct information about the closure.

b *Outstanding certificates* – For a standard-setting body, a closure plan should address the time validity of currently issued certificates and if there is any other body which is assuming responsibility for maintaining the integrity of the certificates.

c   *On-going acknowledgement* – Participating organizations should maintain for a lengthy period of time information on their website about the planned or unplanned closure of any affiliated MSG along with the financial accounting of any organizational assets or unpaid liabilities.

Two questions on financial responsibility

The flow of cash is always a complicated political issue. Cash has a way of making inter-personal, intra-organizational, and inter-organizational management so much more complicated. In this context, "cash" is used to cover direct, indirect, and in-kind payments to fund core activities, including: hosting of meetings; preparation of background papers; compensation for staff time, travel-related expenses, and underwriting organizational programs; and provision of physical office space and other institutional services. The key financial questions quite simply relate to where the cash is coming from and how it is managed inside the MSG to meet its operating expenses and program-related costs.

The institutions providing the cash to finance a group or to underwrite programs expect their views to be given extra weight. Institutions or participants who receive cash payments from a related donor or from the MSG may well have their views influenced by this process. The governance issue is then to ensure that all forms of cash movement are fully disclosed so that member organizations, individual participants, and others outside the MSG can make reasonable political judgements based on verified financial data.

#1 *Where are the resources coming from to pay for the operating expenses of the multistakeholder group, and, separately, where are the resources coming from to finance the programs and/or the recommendations of the multistakeholder group?*

The flow of cash into the multilateral system is described in Chapter 2. While the underlying premise behind the regular budget for multilateral financing is the ability to pay, the net result is that those governments which provide the greatest operational funds have a lopsided political influence on the UN system as a whole. In fact, the major donor countries in the UN have a separate body to review every proposal from the Secretary-General before it even goes to the financial committee of the whole membership of the UN. As the flow of cash from extra-budgetary donors has grown in absolute amounts and relative to regular budgetary cash, foundations, individual corporations, and direct governmental grants have come to exert a disproportionate political influence on the intergovernmental system.

As with the multilateral system, the suppliers of cash can use their financial power to enhance their political and economic leverage. Consequently, decisions about the acceptability of sources of cash and the allocation of cash within the MSG raise democratic governance concerns. Were these decisions made on their merits or on a combination of their merits and the views of the donor? Were the rationales for major decisions provided fully to the leaders and other participants of the MSG and made available for review by those impacted by the actions of the MSG?

The operational funding to support the MSG itself can be raised by having each organization or stakeholder category paying its own costs, by cash support from financially stable participants to cover the costs of other participants, by the UN system or bilateral aid agencies paying expenses for all or most of the participants, by resources from foundation grants, or by income derived from the activities of the MSG. Each of these steps has discrete democratic governance impacts, that can in turn affect the governance of any MSG.

In addition, for MSGs there are atypical financial issues to be addressed, including: (a) what is the principle for internal taxing – progressive or regressive?; (b) how to record properly in-kind and non-financial support in addition to pass-through financial contributions?; (c) what obligations fall on individual stakeholder participants if operating expenses are not met?; (d) can operating debts be incurred by the MSG?, and, (e) if so, what due diligence process is used in evaluating the independence of the lender from individual stakeholder participants?

Basic democratic practices that should be expected:

a *Organizational level disclosure* – The annual budgets and financial accounts of secretariats and the MSG including sources of revenue, income, and in-kind and non-financial expenditures ought to be publicly available at least on an annual basis.
b *Member level disclosure* – The policies for reimbursements or per diem allowances offered to multistakeholder members including the amount of money allowed or offered for reimbursement of per diem allowances and any scales or formulas applied to determine amounts ought to be publicly available.
c *Payments between members, the convener, and/or organizations associated with the multistakeholder group* – Current and past multistakeholder members should be required to disclose any financial or in-kind payments they or members of their families received from the MSG, other multistakeholder members, or other parties which may benefit financially or politically from the outcome of the MSG's actions.

#2 *How are decisions made on where resources will go to underwrite the program as well as to satisfy organizational needs?*

In national governments the preparation of the budget and the approval of the budget can be a long drawn out affair. For the UN, the budget preparation and approval process takes two years and involves the operating office, the UN's internal budget office, a review by a body of the major UN donors, a review by a committee of the UN membership, and finally a vote of the whole membership. The draft budget and the final budget are published on the UN's website.

Each stakeholder in an MSG brings to the group a different history of budget making and a different culture for managing expenditures. The way a corporation makes budget decisions and the way that parliaments make budget decisions are quite different; so too are differences between an international trade union and a community association. One key challenge for the financial governance of an MSG is to decide the approach that will be used to draft the budget proposal, to approve the budget, to review expenditures against the operational budget, to oversee the hiring and firing of staff, and to approve the retention and fees for consultants and other organizational services. As each stakeholder's financial decision system and culture is different, this process is often difficult and not necessarily transparent to all participants and the wider affected community.

Basic democratic practices that should be expected:

a *Original and final organizational budget disclosure* – The proposed and approved budget, including line by line operating expenses, should be made available on the multistakeholder's website.
b *Salaries and benefits* – Salaries and benefits to senior staff and to directors, if they are paid, should be disclosed in annual filings and be available for wider distribution.
c *Consultant fees and rates* – Total fees to consultants and the fees to the largest consultants and their rates should regularly be made available both inside and outside the MSG.
d *Transactions with related parties* – All transactions above a minimum level to parties related to the MSG, to members of the governing body, and to senior staff should be routinely disclosed.

Chapter summary

Translating the concept of democracy into the international arena is difficult at the best of times. Not translating democracy into the international arena – or further limiting the scope of the concept of democracy in a new global governance system – is unhealthy at the best of times. This chapter has identified a number of practical matters that leaders of non-state organizations and public policy scholars may wish to consider about the democratic structure of a particular MSG. Given the complexity of international democracy, there is no doubt that there are even further matters that the leadership of organizations inside an MSG and affected people outside the multistakeholder group should consider in evaluating whether a particular MSG's rules and practices are in accordance with broad principles of democracy.

132 *Decisions around multistakeholder groups*

The questions and the commentary of the thirteen questions discussed here are intended to flesh out the challenges the various issues raise. The following chapter explores further some of the fundamental complexities for global governance presented by multistakeholderism, and suggests some alternative conceptual foundations for the next form of global governance.

Notes

1 For example, the "Eastern European region" consists of countries that formerly were considered under the effective control of the USSR, but many of those countries are now members or candidate members of the EU and the USSR no longer legally exists.
2 For example,

> [The terms of reference] can either be formal or informal. Informal agreements are based on a non-bureaucratic, sometimes only orally expressed, mutual consent. At first sight, they seem to be an attractive solution as they allow for flexibility, for example, to easily terminate partnerships if prospects of success are poor. Moreover, they avoid the complexities of legal procedures which can be compelling if drafting formal agreements would result in high transaction costs, as can be the case once partnerships involve large numbers of small companies from different regions.
>
> (UN 2013: 25)

3 This does not apply to academics, celebrities, ex-public officials, and similarity situated individuals.

References

Brouwer, Herman and Jim Woodhill, with Minu Hemmati, Karen Vershoosel and Simon van Vugt. 2016. "The MSP Guide: How to Design and Facilitate Multi-Stakeholder Partnerships, Second Edition." Bourton on Dunsmore, Rugby, Warwickshire: Centre of Development Innovation of Wageningen University & Research.

Dingwerth, Klaus and Philipp Pattberg. 2009. "World Politics and Organizational Fields: The Case of Transnational Sustainability Governance." *European Journal of International Relations* 15, no. 4: 707–44.

Global Knowledge Partnership. 2003. "Multi-Stakeholder Partnerships Issue Paper." Kuala Lumpur: Overseas Development Institute and Foundation for Development Cooperation.

GoodWeave. n.d. "About." Accessed March 13, 2018. Available from http://skol.org/organization/goodweave-international/.

Gasser, Urs, Ryan Budish, and Sarah West. 2015. "Multistakeholder as Governance Groups: Observations from Case Studies." Cambridge, MA: Berkman Klein Center, Harvard University.

Hemmati, Minu, Felix Dodds, Jasmin Enayati, and Jan McHarry. 2012. *Multistakeholder Processes for Governance and Sustainability: Beyond Deadlock and Conflict*, London: Earthscan.

ICoCA (International Code of Conduct Association). n.d. "History." Accessed April 10, 2018. Available from www.icoca.ch/en/history.

ISEAL. 2017. "State of sustainable markets: Statistics and emerging trends (2017)." London: ISEAL Alliance, International Trade Centre, International Institute for Sustainable Development, Research Institute of Organic Agriculture (FiBL).

Martens, Jens. 2007. *Multistakeholder Partnerships – Future Models of Multilateralism* Global Policy Forum. January 2007.

MSI Integrity. 2015. "Protecting the Cornerstone: Assessing the Governance of EITI (Extractive Industries Transparency Initiative) Multi-Stakeholder Groups." San Francisco, CA: Institute for Multi-Stakeholder Initiative Integrity.

MSI Integrity. 2017. "MSI Evaluation Tool: For the Evaluation of Multi-stakeholder Initiatives v.1.0." San Francisco, CA: Institute for Multi-Stakeholder Initiative Integrity, with the International Human Rights Clinic, Harvard Law School.

WEF. 2016. *Building Partnerships for Sustainable Agriculture and Food Security. A Guide to Country-Led Action*: Geneva: World Economic Forum, prepared in collaboration with Deloitte Consulting.

WHO. 2003. "Who Framework Convention on Tobacco Control." Geneva: World Health Organization.

WHO. 2017. *Engagement with Non-State Actors: Report by the Director General*. Provisional Agenda Item 5.5, WHO Doc. EB 142/28 (November 27, 2017).

UN. 2013. *UN-Business Partnerships: A Handbook*' New York: United Nations Global Compact and Global Public Policy Institute.

UNECE. 2008. "Guidebook on Promoting Good Governance in Public-Private Partnerships." New York and Geneva: United Nations Economic Commission for Europe.

6 Where can we go from here?

The current state of play

Anthropomorphic impacts on the world's ecology are not being managed; the global governance of military power is dysfunctional; and the massive imbalance in control of wealth is not even on the global agenda. After the military-economic-ethnic catastrophes of World War I and World War II, a plan was put in place to address the governance failures of the day. Today's governance failures invite a similar response.

This challenge has been taken up by a variety of international bodies: the expert-oriented Commission on Global Governance (The Commission on Global Governance 1995), the government-led resolutions on global governance (UN 2011), the corporate-driven 2010 GRI (WEF 2010), and the foundation-inspired 2018 Global Challenge Prize (The Global Challenges Foundation n.d.). These proposals, along with others by scholars, practitioners in the field of global affairs, and citizens from all regions, are being examined. With this combined effort, the international community has an opportunity to build a global democratic governance plan for the next fifty years that draws on a broad array of political energy and experiences.

Multistakeholderism today is being presented as a fix for global governance chasms. It is offered as a way to manage a myriad of small and large risks in local areas and around the globe and has a wonderful appeal. It explicitly or implicitly says that governments, international organizations, TNCs, civil society, and a host of other actors can work together. It further advocates that, if these powerful social forces work well together, multistakeholderism may be the system that discovers solutions for present and future global crises. It takes the view that corporate effectiveness and efficiency techniques can be meaningfully transferred to the global governance arena. As described more fully in Chapter 2, multistakeholderism is on the global stage as the result of an unusual conjunction of social, economic, and political forces. By asserting that all the relevant actors are invited into the multistakeholder space, it creates the illusion of democracy,

Contemporary multistakeholderism, no matter how it is practiced, rests on some highly risky and clearly non-democratic features. Four of these elements are: the creation of convener-selected or self-selected global governors; the structural asymmetry of power within a multistakeholder group which favors those actors with greater economic, military, or social power outside the multistakeholder group; the lack of avenues for meaningful participation of peoples and communities who discover they are affected by a multistakeholder group; and the structural omission of any dispute resolution platform to challenge the direction of a multistakeholder group. On the psychological and organizational side, there is, for some participants in multistakeholder groups, seemingly a rush to be designated as a "global governor" without formally having to acknowledge the new role. Likewise, the transition in roles, described in more detail in Chapter 3, applies across the spectrum of institutions that are seeking to replace the nation-state as the exclusive leader in international relations.

Policy-oriented multistakeholderism can take topics off the agenda of the UN system and move them under its umbrella. Conversely, the UN system can shift unresolved global crises over to multistakeholder groups. There are strong reasons why leading actors in policy-oriented multistakeholder groups are likely to re-fashion the UN system's scoping and perception of the issue. Global standard-setting multistakeholder groups have been created to provide the ethical, environmental, and social values in global product markets that OECD governments and TNCs have made sure that multilateralism will not do. High-impact technology standard-setting MSG move decision-making away from national hearings and potential regulatory interventions and even by-pass the ISO. Project-oriented multistakeholder groups gain their status in international and national affairs in large part because elected governments have left so many public needs un-met that it is impacting the overall legitimacy of democracy. The net result is that each issue that is handled by a multistakeholder group significantly weakens multilateralism and national aspirations for a healthy and robust democratic society.

Multistakeholderism suits certain non-state actors as they assume that political obligations, liabilities, and responsibilities in international affairs will remain with the nation-states. In more recent decades, the international community has also evolved definitions and practices for accountability, transparency, and international public participation. These concepts provide the conceptual and practical basis for the contemporary international rule of law. For powerful multistakeholder organizations such as the WEF, the international rule of law is just a matter that can be set aside when it gets in the way of a multistakeholder consensus. But it is an illusion to think that global governors, as the partial replacement of ministries and departments of foreign affairs, will forever be immune to some elements of what are currently state obligations, state responsibilities, and state liabilities.

At the heart of the governance case for a multistakeholder world are claims that it increases international public participation. With many more categories of organization explicitly involved in global governance, multistakeholderism elevates international public participation well beyond that which operates in multilateralism. However, each category of participants is not necessarily treated equally inside or outside the multistakeholder group. The asymmetric external and internal balance of power within the multistakeholder group is reflected in the relative lack of attention to rules, protections, and platforms for minority or weaker participants and the relative lack of means for external actors who are impacted by a multistakeholder group's actions to appeal against the direction and control of the multistakeholder project. In this sense, the increased numbers of types of participants does not translate into meaningful international public participation.

Multistakeholderism: additional structural limitations

In addition to these challenges to democracy, multistakeholderism has sidestepped a number of crucial governance issues. Global governance requires a stable, long-term institutional basis. One of the organizational beliefs, as presented in Chapter 4, is that participation in multistakeholderism is voluntary. The voluntary nature, and therefore the temporary basis of each multistakeholder group, makes it difficult to envision a long-term institutional foundation. For some types of multistakeholder groups, volunteerism may enhance their appeal to governments, who don't wish to see any acknowledged diminution of their claim to exclusive status in international relationships; it may also enhance their appeal to the international corporate community, who have grown over-accustomed to relative autonomy from any formal governance in international markets; and it may similarly enhance their appeal to other constituencies, who don't want to recognize the potential political and social obligations and liabilities that may follow from joining in a multistakeholder arrangement as global governors. The exception here is the MSG governance of new ground-breaking high-impact technologies, where market self-interest has prompted a more stable governance system.

To manage the globe requires a vast amount of cash and assets. Yet multistakeholderism has avoided addressing any of the challenges of a new system of global taxation or a new mechanism to control the flow of classes of high-risk assets. This is ironic, as it was the start of the current recession by a financial crisis that prompted the WEF to undertake its ground-breaking GRI study. Multistakeholderism has chosen instead to leave funding matters in the hands of market-based instruments, such as the pricing of ecosystem services or devising new ways for a project-focused multistakeholder undertaking to charge for water or other vital human needs. Project-based multistakeholder groups have joined other development-oriented projects to reach out for government funding from aid budgets or to request exemptions from tax obligations. Standard-setting multistakeholder projects expect that heightened social and ecological standard costs can largely be passed on to consumers rather than force firms in their related sectors to internalize the costs that they have externalized around the globe. In the UN system, the taxing system is premised on the concept that each country should pay for intergovernmental services in accordance with its ability to pay, yet no multistakeholder group has institutionalized this ability-to-pay approach to implement its goals or programs.

The world has enormous military, police, private security, and non-state armed forces that need to be managed. A major driver for the creation of the League of Nations was WWI; a major driver for the UN system was WWII. Any new global governance system has to have the potential ability to manage the vast store of war-making technologies and war-invested institutions in order to avoid a World War III. Multistakeholderism has not grappled with any effort to have multiple stakeholders governing national militaries or other armed conflicts.[1]

Next steps on the governance of multistakeholderism

If the momentum toward multistakeholderism continues, there are a good number of steps that should be taken to enhance the democratic characteristics of multistakeholder groups and to place democratic concerns more clearly on the agenda of multistakeholderism. These steps include:

a   opening a political space to re-define the core principles of responsibility, obligation, and liability in international relations whenever a multistakeholder group is used to address a global or regional issue;
b   adopting a stop-look-and-wait attitude to all new proposals for multistakeholder groups until a thorough due diligence review is carried out of the democratic governance elements as well as the effectiveness and efficiency assertions about any new multistakeholder group;
c   building stable multistakeholder organizations without the institutional uncertainty of volunteerism;
d   undertaking long-term research on multistakeholder claims to democracy, the role of the convener, and the assessment of claims to effectiveness and efficiency in global governance;
e   hosting open discussions on the minimal standards necessary for multistakeholder rule books and drafting a convention which formalizes the relevant parts of these minimal standards;
f   creating a public forum which can function as a judicial court to provide those excluded from a multistakeholder process an opportunity to seek appropriate remedies and those who are adversely impacted to seek appropriate compensation; and
g   establishing a global repository for all multistakeholder terms of reference, reports of financial income and financial expenses, donors, conflict of interest statements, and waivers.

138 *Where can we go from here?*

As Chapter 2 has argued, contemporary multistakeholderism is an outgrowth of a number of different political, economic, institutional, and competing forces. Some of these same forces have opened up other options for the next phase of global governance.

Next steps on global democratic governance

This section describes three other potential candidates for the next phase of global governance, each of which has a stronger institutional claim to having a democratic core. Whether any of the following three approaches is the best or most reasonable next organizing principle for global governance is not really relevant. What is relevant is that the democratic characteristics of multistakeholderism should also be evaluated in comparison with other candidate systems of global governance.

There is time to avoid drifting into multistakeholder governance as the next phase of global governance. As with the end of WWI and the end of WWII, it is opportune to think about how to institutionalize under-governed political international space and to build institutions that can deliver a socially and environmentally healthy planet. The international community has grown accustomed to work on the global governance of specific sectors (i.e., global governance of health and global governance of the food system). What is now required is to move this up a notch and work directly on the global governance of globalization.

Re-constituting multilateralism

With 193 government actors in the multilateral system, a key number of these nation-states may propose a new dynamic that shifts both their leadership capacity and willingness to tackle core structural under-governed issues in their region or under-managed global crises. The political economic rationale for a potential re-construction of multilateralism is that the other options are too uncomfortable to accept: that multistakeholderism will displace governments, and that non-action on major regional and global issue will further weaken national elites and the nation-state in managing domestic realities. Tentative steps in this re-construction can be seen in the initial efforts to create the BRIC alliance, to create regional financing institutions, to shift the basis for global reference currencies from the dollar to a basket of currencies, and to pool efforts to protect cross-border natural ecosystems against climate change and other powerful anthropogenically driven ecological forces.

Many of the steps that could be taken to re-constitute multilateralism are rather straightforward to describe.

On the political side, the UN system could:

a   open negotiations on a new way to manage the planet's ecological stability, particularly covering the oceans and other globally important

Where can we go from here? 139

natural resources. This new approach should establish a secure regional or global governance system that can legitimately distribute the risks and benefits from parts of the planet that are "outside" the reach of land-based boundaries;
b   form a new global intergovernmental institution above existing intergovernmental organizations and commercial enterprises with the single task of reversing wealth and social inequalities;
c   grapple with a global taxing formula for global governance based on the realities of the financialization of globalization, whose revenues should underwrite the funding of international organizations to function properly and address the tasks in (b) above; and
d   establish a global registry and a standardized disclosure format for all actors involved in globalization. National and sub-national registration of businesses and other actors is out of sync with the realities of a globalized economy.

On the structural side, the UN system could:

a   institutionalize active multi-constituency consultative processes for all intergovernmental bodies and their secretariats;
b   create formal standing congresses of civil society organizations, parliamentarian bodies, and corporate, religious, and science bodies to advise the General Assembly and other intergovernmental bodies;
c   codify (a) and (b) into a new Vienna Convention on Rights and Obligations for Multi-Constituency Participation in Global Governance;
d   formally link all currently autonomous intergovernmental bodies under one general assembly;
g   establish direct digital links between the UN system's intergovernmental meetings to respective national ministries, by-passing the bottlenecks of local missions and national foreign offices;
h   arrange for a commonly trained and equipped military force to intervene in contested violent regions;
i   repair the lopsided voting arrangements in the Security Council and other specialized councils and organizations; and
j   coordinate the funding of high-level global policy research bodies on evolving global challenges, modelled in part on the Intergovernmental Panel on Climate Change.

The combination of these specific changes would put multilateralism back in the forefront of global governance. What is relevant is that there are a good number of institutional structural changes that could radically transform multilateralism, were nation-states collectively willing to replace WWII-style multilateralism with a framework that could address a greater proportion of today's risks and challenges.

Directly governing diverse power sources

A second possible direction for a future global governance system would be to recognize that there are four relatively autonomous power centers in the world today, and that they will not relinquish what they perceive as their relative power without seeing clear benefits in doing so, or without a degree of coercion. Governments, TNCs, international civil society organizations, and the world's people all have different foundations of power that could justify their separate claims to participate in global governance. What is missing is an institutional arrangement that allows the conflicting and cooperating elements of these four centers of power to work out how to govern the planet within a democratic framework. This model could be based on a four-chamber parliamentary system with an associated international court system. The model here is that the House of Commons in the UK was created to counterbalance the House of Lords, as was the US House of Representatives as a citizen-based counterweight to the state-based Senate.

In a four-chamber parliamentary system there could be one chamber for governments; two chambers – each with a similar structure – for multinational corporations and international civil society organizations; and one chamber for the direct engagement of individuals in global governance using the availability of an internet-connected world to make global public decisions. The government chamber could combine the existing UN General Assembly with the governing bodies of the other international agencies and programs, while the TNC and the international civil society chambers could have sub-chambers for key constituencies which would elect members to their full sector chamber. Each chamber and sub-chamber could autonomously develop public policy and programs on their own and have a solid procedural route to engage the other power centers for building inter-chamber agreements. This iterative inter-chamber decision-making system could be designed to overcome key failures in contemporary global governance.

A new organizing unit for global governance

A third possible direction could be the re-conceptualization of international relations by re-asserting that the fundamental basis for democracy is the individual, the citizen, the person. This direction would abandon or downplay pre-existing institutional barriers created to keep the citizen, the person, and the individual apart from each other. This approach could select a new core constituency or a new organizing concept to replace the nation-state as the underlying social basis for global governance. Whether the criteria it is based on are worker, ethnic, gender, or ecosystems, a new working principle would shift the democratic character of governance away from the current indirect multilateral system into one with a more direct engagement that is reflected in a different core principle.

It does not matter if this re-conceptualization of global governance involves a new form of global citizen-to-citizen decision-making without the intermediation of the state, a new form of global worker-to-user decision-making without the centrality and intermediation of business, or a new form of community-to-community decision-making unrestricted by pre-existing barriers institutionalized by race, cultural, or religious organizations; it is worth exploring these alternative terrains for the re-legitimation and re-establishment of democracy and effectiveness in global governance.

Each of these potential re-conceptualizations has microcosms in today's world as reflected in fair trade and cooperative organizations that seek to re-construct the relationship between producer and user, in extra-nation-state elections reflected in the European Parliament, in citizen diplomacy and in cross-cultural living and travel services that aspire to change the way people-to-people decisions could be made, and in the multiculturalism of music, diet, and migration support efforts.

Concluding observations

Multistakeholderism has a number of creative features. Amongst these are that it sponsors an amazing number of experimental global governance structures; it moves beyond the nation-state-based governance system; it welcomes into global governance a range of social actors that contemporary governments are marginalizing; and it offers TNCs a way to engage more openly in global governance. However, no "stakeholder-" based governance system comes close to matching the legitimacy and sense of public participation which has existed for centuries in a "citizen-" based and "nation-state-" based governance system. The very vagueness of who is and who is not a "stakeholder" for individual MSGs means that multistakeholderism as a whole offers a tenuous and illusionary version of democracy. In many ways the practices of contemporary "multistakeholder" governance projects too, as evidenced in this book, are largely retrograde when measured against the practices of democracy that currently operate in national democracies and in the multilateral system. For yet another example, in no national democracy does the commercial sector have a formal role in a national parliament.

For students of democratic global governance, the problematique is then how to conceptualize the governance of globalization, the management of the planet's ecology, and the alleviation of global inequities in a democratic manner. The most widely considered system on the table now, multistakeholderism, does not have the capacity to be that new global governance system. What it does do is to posit that there will be a successor to multilateralism, and in so doing it opens the door for the consideration of a system that places public participation and democracy on the same level as – if not above – effectiveness and efficiency as essential elements of a post-nation-state-based governance system.

One cannot ignore that the push for a successor to multilateralism is also coming from the authoritarianism which longs for a heightened concentration of power – maybe an alliance of authoritarian nations – to diminish the status of democracy, assert greater military-style control over impoverished peoples, and reap short-term benefits from the global ecological disequilibria.

Previous significant shifts in systems of global governance have followed from the ashes of major wars, whether it was the world wars of the 20th century or the European wars of the 17th century, What we might learn from history then, is how to orchestrate a global governance transition in the face of authoritarian forces and without the devastation of a major war. The starting point for this transition is to imagine the new social forces, the new economic institutions, and the new environmental and gender drivers that shift the very locus of the global governance narrative and the global alliances of these forces.

Note

1 Two minor exceptions, as discussed earlier, are the International Code of Conduct for Private Security Providers' Association and the Kimberly Process Certification Scheme.

References

The Commission on Global Governance. 1995. *Our Global Neighbourhood.* Oxford: Oxford University Press.

The Global Challenges Foundation. n.d. "Our Approach." Accessed December 12, 2017. Available from https://globalchallenges.org/en/about/background.

WEF. 2010. "Global Redesign: Strengthening International Cooperation in a More Interdependent World." Geneva: World Economic Forum.

UN. 2011. *The United Nations in Global Governance.* GA Agenda Item 120, UN GA 65th session, UN Doc. A/RES/65/94 (distributed January 28, 2011; adopted December 8, 2010).

Index

Page numbers in **bold** denote tables.

A Guide for National ICT Policy Animators **91**
access to information 113–14
Accord on Fire and Building safety in Bangladesh **24**
accountability 97–8, 122
Adam, L. 65, 69
Alliance for Affordable Internet 70
Alliance for Responsible Mining **91**
Alliance for Water Stewardship **24**
Annan, K. 36, 47
authoritarianism 33–4
authority, locus of 73
autonomy 56, 58

background and development: authoritarianism 33–4; context and overview 28; dysfunctionality of multilateralism 30–3; elite international bodies 45–6; macro political-economic factors 29–34; major international crises 29–30; multi-constituency consultations 47–8; new political platform 48–9; recognition of multistakeholderism as form of governance 42–8; relationship between NGOs/CSOs and the UN system 37–8; "stakeholder" as a concept of governance 42–4; structural transformations 34–42; success of first movers 46–7; summary and conclusions 48–9; transformation of corporate beliefs 40–2; UN and TNCs 34–6
Bali Principles Governing the Management of Multistakeholder

ICT Partnerships for Sustainable Development **91**, 119–20
Bernstein, S. 20
Better Biomass **67**
Better Cotton Initiative 20
bias, organizational 75
bilateral investment treaties 41
boundaries, creation of 8
Boutros-Ghali, B. 35
Bretton Woods Institutions (BWIs) 55
Business Council for Sustainable Development 35

capital, movement of 4
Cardoso Commission 5, 47, 60
Cardoso, F.H. 5
Carnegie Climate for Geoengineering Governance Initiative **22**
Cashore, B. 20
challenges, of multistakeholderism 10
civil society organizations (CSOs) 14; access to MSGs 75; changing role 74–6; as global actors 59–61; relationship with TNCs 38–40, 74–5; relationship with UN 37–8; status 75–6
closure: community engagement on closure 128–9; internal governance 124–5
Cold War 30
collaboration 64
Commission on Sustainable Development (CSD) 46
Commission on Transnational Corporations 34–6
Committee on Food Security (CFS) **13**, 38

144 *Index*

community engagement on closure 128–9
competition, to collaboration 64
composition of MSGs 113–19; democratic practices 114, 115, 117; diversity 117–19; representation 116–17, 118–19; selection criteria 114–16
conferences, global 30
confidentiality 122, 128
conflict of interest 10–11, 93–5; and transparency 98
constituencies, representation 8
Construction Sector Transparency Initiative 70
Consultative Group on International Agricultural Research (CGIAR) 78
convenors 65–71; choice of stakeholder categories 65–6, 69, 71; selection of MSG members 113–14; terms of reference 119–20
core standard, representative democracy 9
corporate beliefs 40–2
corporate morality 77
corporate personhood 9
corporate social responsibility (CSR) 42–3
costs, externalizing 95–6
credibility 114–15

decision making: accountability 122; closing an MSG 124–5; community engagement on closure 128–9; composition of MSGs 113–19; context and overview 111–13; decision points 111–12; dispute resolution 123–4; engagement 125–6; equitable 92–3; external responsibilities 125–9; and financial resources 129–30; financial responsibility 129–31; internal governance 119–25; mode of operation 121–2; resource allocation 130–1; summary and conclusions 131–2; terms of reference 119–21
democracy: and global governance gaps 6–7; representative 7–10
democratic challenges 53
democratic legitimacy 11–12
democratic practices: closure 124–5; community engagement on closure 128–9; composition of MSGs 114, 115, 117, 118–19; dispute resolution 123–4; engagement 125–6; financial resources 129–30; mode of operation 122; reporting and disclosure 126–8; resource allocation 131; terms of reference 121
democratic standards, and global governance 5–6
democratic theory: individual as core unit 6; representation 53–4
Dingwerth, K. 39, 96, 121–2
disclosure 126–8; financial resources 129–30
dispute resolution 123–4
diverse power sources, governing 140
diversity, composition of MSGs 117–19
domestic economic management 32–3
donors 78; leverage 129–30
dual oversight model, replacement government in failed states 107–8
due diligence 114–15

e-commerce rules 41
Economic and Social Council (ECOSOC) 37
economic think-tanks 55
efficiency and effectiveness 95–7, 111
elected council model 102–3
elite international bodies 45–6
engagement 125–6
environmental and social standard-setting MSGs 19–20, **20**, 23
environmental impact statements 88
equality, of nation states 2
Ethical Trade Initiative 70
external responsibilities 125–9; community engagement on closure 128–9; confidentiality 128; engagement 125–6; reporting and disclosure 126–8

financial crises 29; Global Recession 4, 36, 76–7
financial institutions, interconnectedness 41
financial responsibility 129–31; resource allocation 130–1; resources 129–30
Financing for Development Conference 36
first movers, success of 46–7
Food and Agriculture Organization (FAO) 35, 55; Committee on Food Security (CFS) **13**, 38
funding, and taxation 136–7

Index 145

future: governing diverse power sources 140; next steps on governance 137–41; organizational units 140–1; state of play 134–6; structural limitations 136–7; summary and conclusions 141–2
future re-constituting multilateralism 138–9

Gasser, U. 98, 127
gatekeepers 65
gender balance 5, 118
General assembly Resolution on Partnerships for Development 91
Generalized Agreement on Tariffs and Trade (GATT) 55
Geneva Conventions 54
geographical balance 5–6
geopolitical balance 117–18
global actors: category assignment 75; category boundaries 75; civil society organizations (CSOs) 74–6; context and overview 52–3; convenors 65–71; donors 78; governance under multilateralism 57–8; institutional foundations 53–63; intergovernmental bodies and secretariats 58; intergovernmental structures 55–7; multilateralism and non-state actors 59; multistakeholder categories 67; multistakeholder categories, diversity 70–1; nation-state actors 71–3; new actors 63–79; NGOs/CSOs 59; other non-state actors 78–9; potential multistakeholder categories 68; power asymmetry 64; private sector 61–3, 76–7; self-perception 64–5; state actors 71–3; TNCs as crucial 62–3; transition from multilateralism to multistakeholderism 63–5; UN secretariats 73–4
Global Agenda Council on the Arctic 18
Global Alliance for Improved Nutrition 24
Global Compact 36, 87, 102
global conferences 30
global e-commerce rules 41
global ecology, and multilateralism 3
global finance, and multilateralism 4
Global Future Councils 9
global governance: and democratic standards 5–6; gaps, and democracy 6–7; institutional foundations 53–63; *see also* governance
Global Governance 2025 report 85
global inequalities, and multilateralism 4–5
Global Network Initiative 70
Global Partnership for Business and Biodiversity 22
Global Partnership for Effective Development Co-operation 91
Global Partnership for Oceans 19
global problems, unsolved 84–6
Global Recession 4, 36, 76–7
Global Redesign Initiative (GRI) 9, 41, 45–6, 72, 74, 77, 84, 95, 106, 107
Global Reporting Initiative 15, 67
Global Sustainable Tourism Council 20, 70
global taxation 136–7
Global Water Partnership 88
globalization: challenges to 76–7; monitoring 41; and quasi-state global institution 40–1
Golf Environmental Organization 70
governance: diverse power sources 140; effects of multistakeholderism 1; explorers 64; under multilateralism 57–8; next steps on 137–41; participatory 8, 135–6; re-constituting multilateralism 138–9; units of 86–7; *see also* global governance
governing councils: elected from stakeholders 102–3; multi-chamber advisory model 103–4
grievance mechanisms 123–4
Growing Inclusive Markets Initiative 35

Hague Conference of the Parties to the Convention on Biodiversity 73
hard law 54
human rights, roles of NGOs/CSOs 61
Hydropower Sustainability Assessment Protocol 67

identity categorization, MSGs 6
implementation, outsourcing of 48
individuals: as organizational units 140–1; as representatives 89–90
inequality: effects of 76; increase in 29; within MSGs 14; reduction 30
information, access to 113–14
Initiative for Responsible Mining Assurance 20

146 *Index*

institutional foundations 53–63
institutional responsibility 15
inter-country relations 56
interconnectedness, financial institutions 41
intergovernmental bodies, and secretariats 58
intergovernmental structures 55–7
internal governance 119–25; closing an MSG 124–5; confidentiality 122; decision making 121–2; dispute resolution 123–4; rule book 122; terms of reference 119–21
internal structure 16
International Council of Toy Industries (ICTI) Care **20**
International Finance Corporation 35
international governing bodies, one-institution image 31–2
International Labour Organization (ILO) 57
international market, uniqueness 40
International Organization for Standardization (ISO) 17, 19, 21, 44, 48, 57–8, 63, 93
international project-oriented MSGs 23, **24**
International Seafood Sustainability Foundation **20**
International Social and Environmental Accreditation and Labelling Alliance (ISEAL) 18, 93
International Telecommunication Union (ITU) 21
International Union for Conservation of Nature (IUCN) 58, **70**
Internet Corporation for Assigned Names and Numbers (ICANN) 21, **22**, 46, 72, **88**, 93
internet governance 21
Internet Governance Forum 21

Kimberly Process Certification Scheme 17, **18**, 46–7

language, and accessibility 119
law: hard law 54; soft law 54, 106–7
legitimacy: and accountability 97–8; achieving 113; democratic 11–12; guard of 65; of MSGs 84; stakeholders 86; TNCs 76
leverage, donors' 129–30

Ma, J. 41

macro political-economic factors 29–34; authoritarianism 33–4; dysfunctionality of multilateralism 30–3; major international crises 29–30; nation states' weakness 32–3
Major Groups 37–8
major international crises 29–30
market-based economics, adoption of 2–3
meetings, openness 128
military alliances 55
Millennium Development Goals (MDGs) 29
Millennium Report (Annan) 47
mining industry 39
mode of operation 121–2
multi-chamber advisory model 103–4
multi-constituency consultations 12–13, 47–8; mis-labelling **13**; shift to multistakeholder governance 14–16
multilateralism: changes affecting 2; dysfunctionality of 30–3; and global ecology 3; and global finance 4; and global inequalities 4–5; governance under 57–8; re-constituting 138–9; structural limitations 2–5
multistakeholder categories: balance 69; boundaries 75; category assignment 75; choice of 65–6, 69, 71; diversity 67, 70–1; potential categories **68**
multistakeholder groups (MSGs): challenges of 10; closing 124–5; composition 113–19; gender balance 5; geographical balance 5–6; identity categorization 6; internal structure 16; legitimacy 84; limitations of democracy 8; membership 7–8; policy-oriented MSGs 16–17, **18–19**; potential scope 9; power 9–10, 14; product and process-oriented MSGs 17–23; project-oriented MSGs 23–5, **24**; role of governments 72–3; types 16–25; United Nations 15–16
multistakeholderism: as form of governance 42–8; reasons for adopting 1–2; "stakeholder" as a concept of governance 42–4; *see also* background and development

nation-state actors 71–3
nation states: centrality of 56–7; features 2; relations between 53–5; roles in multilateral system 65; weakness 32–3

national governments, perceptions of multistakeholderism 9–10
Natural Capital Coalition 67
natural resources 39
Network of Global Future Councils 17, 77
new technology MSGs 21–3, **22**
New Vision for Agriculture Initiative 70
no-growth budgets 30
non-democratic features 134–5
non-governmental organizations (NGOs): as global actors 59–61; power 14–15; relationship with UN 37–8
non-stakeholders 86
non-state actors 59
non-state global leadership 47–8
North–South inter-regional battles 30

one-big-table model 99–100
one-country-one-vote principle 9
one-institution image, international governing bodies 31–2
openness 97–8
Organization for Economic Cooperation and Development (OECD) 4; and TNCs 35, 62
organizational beliefs: context and overview 83, **84**; efficiency and effectiveness 95–7; equitable decision making 92–3; and governance consequences 84–98; identification of stakeholders 87–9; individuals as representatives 89–90; managing conflicts of interest 93–5; position of non-stakeholders 86; stakeholder as governance category 86–7; stakeholder participation 87–9, **88**; summary and conclusions 108; transparency 97–8; unsolved global problems 84–6; volunteerism 90–2, **91**
organizational bias 75
organizational models: governing councils elected from stakeholders 102–3; multi-chamber advisory model 103–4; one-big-table model 99–100; parallel leadership model 106–7; replacement government in failed states 107–8; secretariat-led groups 104–6; summary and conclusions 108; weighted decision making 100–2
organizational units 140–1
outsourcing, of implementation 48

parallel leadership model 106–7
Paris Conference of the Parties to the UNFCCC 73
participatory governance 8, 135–6
Partnership Office 105
Pattberg, P. 39, 96, 121–2
performance gap 106
personhood 9
policy-oriented MSGs 16–17, **18–19**; risky features 135; role of governments 72–3
political-economic factors: authoritarianism 33–4; dysfunctionality of multilateralism 30–3; macro political-economic factors 29–34; major international crises 29–30; nation states' weakness 32–3
Potts, A. 1
poverty reduction 30
power: access to 116; balance 69; extent of 116; within MSGs 14–15
power asymmetry 64; and terms of reference 120; UN secretariat leadership model 105–6
power differentials 108
private sector 61–3; changing role 76–7
problem solving 14
product and process-oriented MSGs 17–23; environmental and social standard-setting MSGs 19–20, **20**, 23; new technologies 21–3, **22**
project-based multistakeholder projects 39, 136
project-oriented MSGs 23–5; authority of members 71; international 23, **24**; role of governments 72–3; task-focused 23–5
public acceptance 1
public-private partnerships (PPPs) 23–5, 35, 39, 62–3, 73, 77, 92, 96; conflict of interest 11; for government 107–8

quasi-state global institution, and globalization 40–1

recognition of multistakeholderism as form of governance 42–8; elite international bodies 45–6; multi-constituency consultations 47–8; non-state global leadership 47–8; "stakeholder" as a concept of governance 42–4; success of first movers 46–7

148 *Index*

recommendations: governance 137–41; governing diverse power sources 140; organizational units 140–1; re-constituting multilateralism 138–9; summary and conclusions 141–2
Renewable Policy Network for the twenty-first century **18**
replacement government in failed states 107–8
reporting 126–8
representation: composition of MSGs 116–17; democratic theory perspective 53–4
representative democracy 7–10; core standard 9
resource allocation, decision making 130–1
resources 129–30
responsibility, institutional 15
rights-based constituencies, representation 8
Rio Conference on Environment and Development 35, 37
risky features 134–5
Roll Back Malaria **24**, 70
rule book, decision making 122
rule of law, effects of multistakeholderism 10–12

Schwab, K. 43
SE4All partnership 105
secretariat-led groups 104–6
selection criteria 114–16
self-perception 64–5
self-regulation 40–1
Singh, P.J. 41–2
social communities, representation 8
soft law 54, 106
sovereignty 2, 4–5
specific non-human constituencies, representation 8
stakeholder: as a concept of governance 42–4; as governance category 86–7; personhood 9
stakeholder participation, organizational beliefs 87–9, **88**
stakeholders: identification of 87–9; legitimacy 86
standard setting groups 39; exclusion of governments 72; NGOs/CSOs 61; passing on costs 136–7; TNC participation 76–7
state actors, changed role 71–3
statecraft 54

Strong, M. 35, 37
structural characteristics: context and overview 83–4, 99; governing councils elected from stakeholders 102–3; multi-chamber advisory model 103–4; one-big-table model 99–100; parallel leadership model 106–7; replacement government in failed states 107–8; secretariat-led groups 104–6; summary and conclusions 108; weighted decision making 100–2
structural limitations 136–7
structural transformations 34–42; corporate beliefs 40–2; relationship between CSOs and TNCs 38–40; relationship between NGOs/CSOs and the UN system 37–8; UN and TNCs 34–6
Sustainable Development Goals (SDGs) 29, 36, 48; energy 105
Sustainable Energy for All **24**

task-focused project-oriented MSGs 23–5
tax jurisdiction shopping 4
taxation 136–7
terminology 16, 28; international governing bodies 31–2; stakeholder terminology 42–3
terms of reference 119–21; democratic practices 121
The Factories of the Future **67**
The First Forty Years (Schwab) 43
The FramingNano Project **22**
The Future of International Governance, Public-Private Cooperation & Sustainable Development group 17
The Global Challenges Foundation 96–7
The Global Fund to Fight AIDS, Tuberculosis and Malaria **24**
The Global Polio Eradication Initiative **24**
Tobacco Convention 36
Toilet Board Coalition **24**
trans-national corporations (TNCs): changing role 76–7; as global actors 62–3; growth and power 2–3; in international market 61–2; and jurisdictional boundaries 4; and OECD 35; relationship with CSOs 38–40, 74–5; standard setting 76–7; and UN 34–6

transparency 97–8, 127
Type II outcomes 36, 46
types, of MSGs 16–25

UN Centre on Transnational Corporations (UNCTC) 34–6
UN Economic and Social Council (ECOSOC) 37
UN High Level Political Forum 13
UN secretariat leadership model 104–6
UN secretariats, changing role 73–4
UN system 56; changing role 73–4; risky features 135; secretariats 58; semi-permanent structures 60; and TNCs 62–3
United Nations: critiques of 30–1; MSGs 15–16; neutrality 58; outsourcing of implementation 48; Partnership Office 105; relationship with NGOs/CSOs 37–8; role 30; rules 54–5; and TNCs 34
United Nations Conference on Trade and Development (UNCTAD) 35–6
United Nations Industrial Development Program (UNDP) 35
United Nations Environment Programme (UNEP) 55
United Nations Forum on Forests 13
units of governance 86–7
units of government 52–3
units of organization 140–1
unsolved global problems 84–6
US Joint Intelligence Agency report 61–2

Utting, P. 40–1

Vienna Conventions 54
volunteerism 11–12, 64, 90–2, **91**, 136
voting mechanisms: one-big-table model 100; weighted decision making 101–2

weighted decision making 100–2
West, J. 59
Westphalia peace conference 2
Westphalian global order 4, 56–7
Wikipedia, stakeholder terminology 42
World Bank, International Finance Corporation 35
World Commission on Dams **18**
World Economic Forum (WEF) 9, 21, 41, 43, 106, 107; engagement with multistakeholder-style governance 45; Network of Global Future Councils 17, 77; New Vision for Agriculture Initiative 70
World Economic Forum (WEF) view of volunteerism 90–2
World Health Organization (WHO) 55; Tobacco Convention 36
World Ocean Council **88**
World Summit on the Information Society 21
World Trade Organization (WTO) 48, 55

Zoller, J. 46

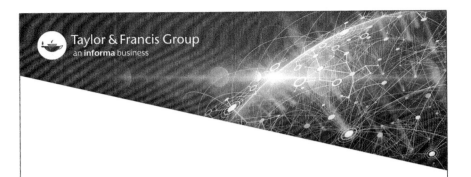